McGraw-Hill Ryerson

PRISM MATH

CANADIAN EDITION

yellow

 **McGraw-Hill
Ryerson**

Toronto Montréal Boston Burr Ridge, IL Dubuque, IA Madison, WI New York San Francisco
St. Louis Bangkok Bogotá Caracas Kuala Lumpur Lisbon London Madrid
Mexico City Milan New Delhi Santiago Seoul Singapore Sydney Taipei

McGraw-Hill

A Division of The McGraw-Hill Companies

Prism Math – Yellow

ISBN: 0-07-096049-6

http://www.mcgrawhill.ca

1 2 3 4 5 6 7 8 9 10   MP   0 9 8 7 6 5

Printed and bound in Canada

Care has been taken to trace ownership of copyright material contained in this text. The publishers will gladly accept any information that will enable them to rectify any reference or credit in subsequent printings.

Library and Archives Canada Cataloguing in Publication

Prism Math – Yellow.

One of a series of non-grade specific workbooks for use in grades 1–12. The level of difficulty increases throughout the series in the following order: gold, brown, red, orange, yellow, green, blue and purple.
ISBN: 0-07-096049-6

1. Mathematics–Problems, exercises, etc. 2. Mathematics–Study and teaching (Elementary) 3. Mathematics–Study and teaching (Secondary)

QA36.5.P755 2005   510'.76   C2005-900451-7

PUBLISHER: Diane Wyman
MANAGER, EDITORIAL SERVICES: Linda Allison
SUPERVISING EDITOR: Kristi Moreau
COPY EDITORS: Julia Cochrane; Write On!
EDITORIAL ASSISTANT: Erin Hartley
PRODUCTION SUPERVISOR: Yolanda Pigden
PRODUCTION COORDINATOR: Janie Deneau
COVER DESIGN: Dianna Little
ELECTRONIC PAGE MAKE-UP: SR Nova Pvt. Ltd., Bangalore, India

COPIES OF THIS BOOK MAY BE OBTAINED BY CONTACTING:

McGraw-Hill Ryerson Ltd.

WEB SITE:
http://www.mcgrawhill.ca

E-MAIL:
orders@mcgrawhill.ca

TOLL-FREE FAX:
1-800-463-5885

TOLL-FREE CALL:
1-800-565-5758

OR BY MAILING YOUR ORDER TO:
McGraw-Hill Ryerson
Order Department
300 Water Street
Whitby, ON L1N 9B6

Please quote the ISBN and title when placing your order.

Student text ISBN:
0-07-096049-6

Contents

YELLOW BOOK PRETESTS 1–12
PROBLEM-SOLVING STRATEGIES
   Multi–Step 13
   Draw a Picture 14
   Look for a Pattern 15
   Guess and Check 16
   Identify Missing Information 17
   Make a Table 18
   Make a List 19
   Solve a Simpler Problem 20
   Work Backward 21
   Estimation 22

1 CHAPTER 1 Addition and Subtraction
      (2–digit through 5–digit)

CHAPTER 1 PRETEST 23
Lessons
 1 Addition Facts 25
 2 Subtraction Facts 26
 3 Addition and Subtraction (2- and 3-digit) . . .27
 4 Addition and Subtraction (3- and 4-digit) . . .29
 5 Addition and Subtraction (4- and 5-digit) . .31
 6 Addition (3 or more numbers) 33
 7 Estimating Sums and Differences 35
CHAPTER 1 PRACTICE TEST 37

2 CHAPTER 2 Multiplication (2–digit
      by 1–digit through 4–digit by 3–digit)

CHAPTER 2 PRETEST 38
Lessons
 1 Multiplication Facts 39
 2 Multiplication (by 1-digit) 41
 3 Multiplication (by 2-digit) 43
 4 Multiplication (by 2-digit) 45
 5 Multiplication (by 3-digit) 47
 6 Estimating Products 49
CHAPTER 2 PRACTICE TEST 51

3 CHAPTER 3 Division
      (2-digit through 4-digit by 1-digit)

CHAPTER 3 PRETEST 52
Lessons
 1 Division Facts 53
 2 Division (by 1-digit) 55
 3 Division with Remainders 57
 4 Checking Division 59
 5 Estimating Quotients 61
CHAPTER 3 PRACTICE TEST 63

4 CHAPTER 4 Division
      (2-digit through 4-digit by 2-digit)

CHAPTER 4 PRETEST 64
Lessons
 1 Division (2-digit) 65
 2 Division (3-digit) 67
 3 Division (3-digit) 69
 4 Division (4-digit) 71
 5 Division (2-, 3-, and 4-digit) 73
CHAPTER 4 PRACTICE TEST 75

5 CHAPTER 5 Division
      (4- and 5-digit by 2-digit)

CHAPTER 5 PRETEST 76
Lessons
 1 Division (5-digit) 77
 2 Division (5-digit) 79
 3 Checking Division 81
 4 Division (4- and 5-digit) 83
CHAPTER 5 PRACTICE TEST 85

6 CHAPTER 6 Money

CHAPTER 6 PRETEST 86
Lessons
 1 Place Value .87
 2 Writing Money 88
 3 Addition of Money 89
 4 Subtraction of Money 91
 5 Multiplication of Money 93
 6 Division of Money 95
 7 Problem Solving 97
CHAPTER 6 PRACTICE TEST 99

7 CHAPTER 7 Graphs and Averages

CHAPTER 7 PRETEST 100
Lessons
 1 Bar Graphs .101
 2 Line Graphs .103
 3 Mean 105
 4 Median, Mode, and Range 107
 5 Probabilities .109
CHAPTER 7 PRACTICE TEST 111

8 CHAPTER 8 Metric Measurement

CHAPTER 8 PRETEST 112
Lessons
 1 Centimetre and Millimetre 113
 2 Perimeter 114

3 Metre and Kilometre 115
4 Units of Length 116
5 Area 117
6 Volume 119
7 Capacity 121
8 Units of Capacity 122
9 Mass 123
10 Units of Mass 124
CHAPTER 8 PRACTICE TEST 125

9 CHAPTER 9 More Metric Measurement

CHAPTER 9 PRETEST .126
Lessons
1 Units of Length .127
2 Perimeter 128
3 Area 129
4 Volume 131
5 Capacity 133
6 Mass 135
CHAPTER 9 PRACTICE TEST 137

10 CHAPTER 10 Fractions

CHAPTER 10 PRETEST 138
Lessons
1 Writing Fractions 139
2 Writing Fractions 140
3 Prime and Composite 141
4 Greatest Common Factor 142
5 Fractions in Simplest Form 143
6 Improper Fractions 145
7 Renaming Numbers 146
8 Mixed Numerals 147
9 Simplest Form 148
CHAPTER 10 PRACTICE TEST 149

11 CHAPTER 11 Multiplication of Fractions

CHAPTER 11 PRETEST 150
Lessons
1 Multiplication (using diagrams) 151
2 Multiplication 152
3 Multiplication 153
4 Multiplication (by whole numbers) 155
5 Multiplication (mixed numerals) 157
6 Multiplication (mixed numerals) 159
7 Multiplication Review 161
CHAPTER 11 PRACTICE TEST 163

12 CHAPTER 12 Addition of Fractions

CHAPTER 12 PRETEST 164
Lessons
1 Addition (fractions) 165
2 Addition (like denominators) 166
3 Addition (like denominators) 167
4 Addition (mixed numerals) 168
5 Renaming Fractions 169
6 Addition (unlike denominators) 171
7 Addition (unlike denominators) 173
8 Addition (mixed numerals) 175
9 Addition Review 177
10 Addition Review 179
CHAPTER 12 PRACTICE TEST 181

13 CHAPTER 13 Subtraction of Fractions

CHAPTER 13 PRETEST 182
Lessons
1 Subtraction (like denominators) 183
2 Subtraction (from whole numbers) 184
3 Subtraction (mixed numerals) 185
4 Subtraction (unlike denominators) 187
5 Subtraction (unlike denominators) 189
6 Subtraction (mixed numerals) 191
7 Subtraction Review 193
8 Subtraction Review 195
CHAPTER 13 PRACTICE TEST 197

14 CHAPTER 14 Geometry

CHAPTER 14 PRETEST 198
Lessons
1 Lines and Line Segments 199
2 Parallel and Perpendicular 200
3 Angles 201
4 Acute, Obtuse, and Right Angles 202
5 Quadrilaterals 203
6 Polygons 204
7 Circles 206
8 Three-Dimensional Objects 207
CHAPTER 14 PRACTICE TEST 208

MID-TEST Chapters 1–9 209–212
FINAL TEST Chapters 1–14 213–216
CUMULATIVE REVIEWS 217–244

ALGEBRA READINESS

Missing Term–Addition 245
Missing Term–Subtraction 246
Missing Term–Multiplication 247
Missing Term–Division 248
Mixed Missing Term 249
Function Tables 250
Number Patterns .252

YELLOW BOOK PRETESTS
Addition Facts (Pretest 1)

	a	*b*	*c*	*d*	*e*	*f*	*g*	*h*
1.	2 +2	5 +3	1 +1	8 +4	7 +1	0 +4	6 +3	3 +2
2.	7 +2	4 +1	6 +4	8 +0	4 +8	3 +7	4 +9	9 +3
3.	6 +5	0 +0	3 +8	8 +3	9 +5	6 +2	9 +0	2 +9
4.	4 +2	1 +3	5 +2	0 +2	9 +4	3 +6	8 +2	4 +7
5.	5 +4	8 +5	6 +6	2 +3	7 +3	2 +1	0 +7	1 +4
6.	9 +6	4 +3	7 +4	3 +5	5 +1	5 +5	8 +9	8 +1
7.	2 +4	9 +2	5 +9	9 +9	6 +7	2 +8	7 +5	4 +6
8.	8 +6	3 +4	2 +5	5 +6	7 +0	7 +6	9 +8	2 +7
9.	7 +9	4 +4	9 +1	6 +8	7 +8	5 +7	3 +9	8 +8
10.	6 +9	9 +7	3 +3	5 +8	2 +6	8 +7	4 +5	7 +7

YELLOW BOOK PRETESTS
Addition Facts (Pretest 2)

	a	*b*	*c*	*d*	*e*	*f*	*g*	*h*
1.	5 +2	1 +3	6 +6	0 +5	4 +0	3 +2	8 +3	2 +4
2.	3 +3	7 +1	2 +1	5 +8	7 +9	4 +4	6 +0	3 +6
3.	4 +3	0 +8	9 +2	7 +8	9 +9	0 +3	6 +7	4 +9
4.	5 +7	8 +4	3 +7	4 +8	6 +2	2 +2	5 +9	1 +1
5.	8 +9	1 +5	0 +0	4 +2	6 +8	8 +5	6 +5	4 +7
6.	2 +5	9 +7	5 +6	8 +2	3 +5	2 +8	9 +3	7 +2
7.	1 +6	6 +3	3 +8	9 +5	5 +5	7 +7	4 +5	2 +9
8.	6 +9	4 +6	8 +7	2 +6	1 +8	9 +8	7 +3	5 +4
9.	7 +5	8 +0	3 +4	7 +4	9 +6	4 +1	0 +9	8 +6
10.	2 +7	8 +8	5 +3	9 +4	3 +9	6 +4	7 +6	1 +9

YELLOW BOOK PRETESTS
Subtraction Facts (Pretest 1)

	a	*b*	*c*	*d*	*e*	*f*	*g*	*h*
1.	6 −5	1 4 −6	7 −2	1 1 −8	9 −4	1 0 −7	7 −6	1 4 −9
2.	9 −7	1 2 −5	7 −5	1 7 −8	8 −8	1 1 −4	6 −3	1 2 −8
3.	6 −6	1 0 −8	9 −2	1 1 −5	6 −2	1 5 −9	8 −6	1 3 −6
4.	1 1 −2	1 6 −7	7 −3	1 2 −9	5 −5	1 1 −7	8 −3	1 2 −4
5.	1 0 −1	1 5 −6	8 −7	1 0 −6	7 −1	1 0 −3	5 −2	1 3 −9
6.	9 −6	1 7 −9	2 −1	1 2 −3	8 −4	1 0 −5	9 −8	1 6 −8
7.	7 −7	1 5 −8	4 −2	1 6 −9	1 −1	1 3 −5	3 −1	1 0 −9
8.	9 −5	1 3 −4	8 −0	1 5 −7	9 −1	1 2 −6	7 −0	1 3 −8
9.	1 1 −3	1 2 −7	8 −1	1 1 −6	9 −0	1 1 −9	8 −5	1 4 −7
10.	1 8 −9	1 0 −4	9 −9	1 3 −7	1 0 −2	1 4 −8	9 −3	1 4 −5

YELLOW BOOK PRETESTS
Subtraction Facts (Pretest 2)

	a	*b*	*c*	*d*	*e*	*f*	*g*	*h*
1.	10 −6	9 −1	11 −3	8 −2	12 −3	5 −0	10 −1	9 −5
2.	11 −7	4 −0	12 −5	10 −9	11 −4	9 −8	13 −4	8 −8
3.	12 −6	9 −7	10 −2	5 −5	12 −8	9 −3	11 −6	6 −0
4.	14 −5	11 −9	12 −4	9 −6	11 −5	8 −1	13 −7	7 −3
5.	12 −7	18 −9	13 −6	6 −6	14 −7	7 −0	11 −2	8 −6
6.	10 −3	9 −2	10 −5	5 −1	13 −8	6 −5	17 −8	7 −1
7.	11 −8	8 −3	12 −9	8 −0	16 −8	8 −7	10 −4	13 −9
8.	10 −7	7 −5	15 −8	6 −2	14 −6	14 −9	15 −7	9 −4
9.	17 −9	6 −1	9 −9	8 −4	15 −9	7 −2	14 −8	8 −5
10.	13 −5	9 −0	16 −9	7 −6	16 −7	10 −8	15 −6	7 −7

YELLOW BOOK PRETESTS
Mixed Facts Pretest

Add, subtract, multiply, or divide. Watch the signs.

	a	*b*	*c*	*d*
1.	63 +4	49 −8	16 ×5	6)48
2.	56 −13	9)37	85 +7	60 ×4
3.	16 ×23	35 +42	7)53	26 −18
4.	5)235	81 ×16	639 −18	507 +41
5.	462 +39	483 −57	23 ×24	4)184
6.	506 −273	70 ×32	7)296	342 +478

	a	*b*	*c*	*d*

7.

a
```
  168
 ×45
```

b
```
  26
  75
  39
 +68
```

c
```
 6392
 −418
```

d
```
14)296
```

8.

a
```
32)278
```

b
```
 7320
 −465
```

c
```
 913
 ×69
```

d
```
  365
  491
  872
 +516
```

9.

a
```
 8070
 −416
```

b
```
  784
 ×123
```

c
```
 6859
 2306
+7174
```

d
```
39)6842
```

10.

a
```
 6943
  872
 1064
+5791
```

b
```
47)15 960
```

c
```
 7000
−5368
```

d
```
  739
 ×105
```

PROBLEM-SOLVING STRATEGIES
Multi-Step

Latoya and Eugene went to the store to buy a birthday present for their dad. They took $30.00 to spend. They bought a pack of golf balls that cost $7.50, a tie that cost $16.25, and a card that cost $1.75. How much money did Latoya and Eugene have left after buying these three items?

What operation do you do first?

They spent __$25.50__ on these three items.

What operation do you do next?

Latoya and Eugene have __$4.50__ left.

First find how much money Latoya and Eugene spent on the three items. To find this amount, **add.**

$$\begin{array}{r} \$7.50 \\ \$16.25 \\ +\$1.75 \\ \hline \$25.50 \end{array}$$

Next find how much money Latoya and Eugene have left. To find this amount, **subtract.**

$$\begin{array}{r} \$30.00 \\ -25.50 \\ \hline \$4.50 \end{array}$$

Solve each problem.

| SHOW YOUR WORK |

1. The Carsons drove from their home in Ottawa, to Halifax, for a vacation. The total distance from Ottawa to Halifax is 1442 km. They drove 409 km on Saturday and 516 km on Sunday. They drove the remaining distance on Monday. How many kilometres did the Carsons drive on Monday?

   What operation do you perform first?_____

   The Carsons drove _____ km on Monday.

2. At the souvenir store, Lee bought three key chains that cost $2.70 each and two T-shirts that cost $14.50 each. How much money did Lee spend at the souvenir store?

   What operation do you perform first? _____

   Lee spent _____ at the souvenir store.

3. Antonio has a garden in his backyard that is 14 m by 4 m. Madeline has a garden in her backyard that is 9 m by 6 m. Whose garden has the larger perimeter? How many metres larger is the perimeter?

   _____ garden perimeter is _____ m larger.

PROBLEM-SOLVING STRATEGIES

Draw a Picture

Camelia is having a party. Counting Camelia, there will be nine people at the party. Camelia is going to order pizza for the party. She wants to order enough pizza so that every person can have up to 3 slices of pizza. If the pizzas each have 8 slices, how many pizzas should Camelia order?

Camelia should order ____4____ pizzas.

Draw pizzas divided into eight slices. Place three 1s in three different slices to represent pizza for one person. Continue this through number 9. Count the number of pizzas needed for the party.

Solve each problem.

SHOW YOUR WORK

1. Tyra has a rectangular garden in her backyard that is 12 m by 10 m. She is going to put a fence around the garden. Between the fence and the garden there will be a 2-m walkway. What is the perimeter of the fence around the garden and walkway?

   The perimeter of the fence will be _____ m.

---

2. Marcus has a roll of plastic table covering that is 2 m wide and 15 m long. He is using it to cover picnic tables at a family picnic. All the picnic tables are 1 m by 3 m. What is the maximum number of picnic tables Marcus can cover with the roll of plastic table covering?

   Marcus can cover up to _____ picnic tables with the plastic table covering.

---

3. Aiyana is filling pages in her scrapbook. Each page of the scrapbook is 28 cm high and 25 cm wide. Each picture is 8 cm by 13 cm. What is the maximum number of pictures that she can fit on one page of her scrapbook?

   Aiyana can fit a maximum of _____ pictures on one page of her scrapbook.

PROBLEM-SOLVING STRATEGIES
Look for a Pattern

In January, Brenda put $10 in her savings account. In February, she put $15 in her savings account. In March, she put $20 in her savings account. If this pattern continues, how much money will Brenda put in her savings account in September?

Each month Brenda puts ____$5____ more in her savings account than the previous month.

In September, Brenda will put ____$50____ in her savings account.

Look for a pattern in the amounts Brenda put into her account in January, February, and March.

January   February   March
  $10 $15 $20
        +$5   +$5

Make a list of the amount she puts in her account each month until September.

Jan.	$10	June	$35
Feb.	$15	July	$40
Mar.	$20	Aug.	$45
Apr.	$25	Sept.	$50
May	$30		

Solve each problem.

SHOW YOUR WORK

1. Ken has tomato plants in his garden. He was able to pick his first tomatoes the first week of summer. That week he picked 4 tomatoes. The second week of summer he picked 5 tomatoes. The third week he picked 7 tomatoes. The fourth week he picked 10 tomatoes. If this pattern continues, how many tomatoes will Ken pick the eighth week of summer?

   In the eighth week of summer, Ken will pick _____ tomatoes.

2. Each birthday Rosa's mother measured her height. On Rosa's second birthday she was 89 cm tall. On her third birthday she was 97 cm tall. On her fourth birthday she was 105 cm tall. If this pattern continues, how tall will Rosa be on her ninth birthday?

   Rosa will be _____ cm tall on her ninth birthday.

PROBLEM-SOLVING STRATEGIES

Guess and Check

Alexis has a total of $75 in her wallet. She has a combination of $5 bills and $10 bills. She has a total of 12 bills. What combination of $5 bills and $10 bills does Alexis have in her wallet?

Alexis has _____9_____ $5 bills in her wallet.

Alexis has _____3_____ $10 bills in her wallet.

The number of bills must total 12.
Take a guess: 6 $10 bills and 6 $5 bills.
   $10 × 6 = $60
   $5 × 6 = $30
   $60 + $30 = $90   Too high
Try again: 2 $10 bills and 10 $5 bills.
   $10 × 2 = $20
   $5 × 10 = $50
   $20 + $50 = $70   Too low
Try again: 3 $10 bills and 9 $5 bills
   $10 × 3 = $30
   $5 × 9 = $45
   $30 + $45 = $75

Solve each problem.

SHOW YOUR WORK

1. Dante has a collection of baseball cards and hockey cards. He has a total of 74 cards in all. He has 10 more baseball cards than hockey cards. How many of each type of card does Dante have in his collection?

   Dante has _____ baseball cards in his collection.

   Dante has _____ hockey cards in his collection.

---

2. Katie is putting a fence around the rectangular garden in her backyard. She needs a total of 42 m of fencing to go all the way around the garden. The length of the garden is twice as long as the width. What is the length and width of Katie's garden?

   The length of Katie's garden is _____ m.

   The width of Katie's garden is _____ m.

PROBLEM-SOLVING STRATEGIES

Identify Missing Information

Over the summer Chayton went to the movie theatre and watched 15 movies. He watched 4 action movies, 5 comedy movies, and the rest were scary movies or science fiction movies. How many scary movies did Chayton watch over the summer?

<u>Not enough information.</u>

Missing information: <u>total number of</u>

<u>science fiction movies Chayton watched</u>

To find the number of scary movies, subtract the number of action, comedy, and science fiction movies from the total number of movies.

$$
\begin{array}{r}
15 \\
-4 \leftarrow \text{action movies}\\
\hline
11 \\
-5 \leftarrow \text{comedy movies}\\
\hline
6 \\
- \text{ number of science fiction}\\
\text{movies}
\end{array}
$$

Information on the number of science fiction movies is missing.

Solve each problem.

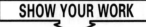
SHOW YOUR WORK

1. Olivia works Monday, Wednesday, Thursday, and Saturday at her part-time job. She works 4 h on Monday and Thursday, and 5 h on Saturday. How many hours does Olivia work each week at her part-time job?

   _____

   Missing information: _____

   _____

---

2. During Saturday's football game, 135 cups of pop were sold at the concession stand. The pop comes in three different sizes: small, medium, and large. They sold 42 small pops, and more large pops than medium pops. How many of each type of pop was sold on Saturday?

   _____

   Missing information: _____

   _____

   _____

PROBLEM-SOLVING STRATEGIES

Make a Table

Bruce is following a recipe to make potato soup. For every three servings he needs two medium potatoes. If Bruce wants to make enough soup for 15 servings, how many medium potatoes does he need?

Bruce will need ____10____ medium potatoes for 15 servings of soup.

Make a table to determine the number of potatoes he will need for 15 servings.

Number of servings	Number of potatoes
3	2
6	4
9	6
12	8
15	10

Solve each problem.

SHOW YOUR WORK

1. Kashana is following a recipe to make pancakes.

   To make 6 pancakes she needs $\frac{1}{2}$ cup of pancake

   mix. How many cups of pancake mix will Kashana need to make 30 pancakes?

   Kashana will need _____ cups of pancake mix to make 30 pancakes.

---

2. A car rental company charged $45 the first day of renting a car and $25 every day after that. Jason rented a car for 5 days from the company. How much did it cost?

   It cost Jason _____ to rent a car for 5 days.

---

3. Bonnie took $20 to the souvenir store. She wants to buy key chains to take home to her family and friends. Each key chain costs $3. What is the maximum number of key chains Bonnie can buy with her money?

   Bonnie can buy a maximum of _____ key chains with her money.

PROBLEM-SOLVING STRATEGIES
Make a List

The jungle tram ride at the amusement park departs every 25 min. The first one of the day leaves at 9:00 A.M. Jasmine and her friends want to get on the jungle tram ride that departs closest to 11:00 A.M. What time will Jasmine and her friends depart on the jungle tram ride?

Jasmine and her friends will depart on the jungle tram ride at __11:05 A.M.__ .

Make a list of the departure times of the jungle tram ride.

9:00 A.M.
9:25 A.M.
9:50 A.M.
10:15 A.M.
10:40 A.M.
11:05 A.M. ← Closest to 11:05 A.M.

Solve each problem.

SHOW YOUR WORK

1. On Sunday, Lenno went for a walk and took a bike ride. He takes a walk every other day and goes for a bike ride every third day. What is the next day that Lenno will do both activities?

   The next day that Lenno will do both activities is _____.

2. Molly is going to paint her kitchen and put up a wallpaper border. For the paint colour, she is deciding between tan and cream. For the border, she is deciding between a flower pattern, a fruit pattern, or a basket weave pattern. How many different combinations of paint and wallpaper border can Molly choose from?

   Molly can choose from _____ different combinations of paint and wallpaper border.

3. For a weekend trip, Dylan packed a blue shirt, a white shirt, and a black shirt. He also packed a denim pair of shorts and a khaki pair of shorts. How many different outfits can Dylan choose from with the clothes he packed?

   Dylan can choose from _____ different outfits.

PROBLEM-SOLVING STRATEGIES

Solve a Simpler Problem

Malcolm spends 5 h 40 min at school every day. He spends 9 h 20 min sleeping every night. How many hours does Malcolm spend at school and sleeping every day?

Malcolm spends ____15____ h at school and sleeping every day.

Adjust the times so you can add simpler numbers. Take the 40 min from 5 h and add to the 20 min to make 1 h. Add the 1 h to 5 h. Use the times 6 h and 9 h to find the total time.

To find the total time, add the two times.

$$6\,h + 9\,h = 15\,h$$

Solve each problem.

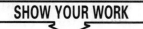

1. Mrs. Kelroy's classroom is 8 m wide and 10 m long. Mr. Price's classroom is 7 m wide and 10 m. How many square metres larger is Mrs. Kelroy's classroom than Mr. Price's classroom?

Mrs. Kelroy's classroom is _____ m² larger than Mr. Price's classroom.

---

2. Dean went shopping at a department store to buy some clothes. He took $50.00 with him. He wanted to buy a pair of shorts that cost $17.99, a T-shirt that cost $11.49, and cologne that cost $22.65. Did Dean have enough money to buy all three items?

Dean _____ have enough money to buy all three items.

PROBLEM-SOLVING STRATEGIES

Work Backward

Jontell went shopping at the mall with some of her friends. She bought a hat that cost $9.45 and a sweatshirt that cost $20.64. After she bought these two items she had $4.91 left. How much money did Jontell take to the mall?

Jontell took __$35.00__ to the mall.

Work backward: Start with the amount left, $4.91, then add the amounts for the hat and the sweatshirt.

$4.91
20.64
+9.45
_____
$35.00 ← beginning amount

Solve each problem.

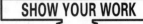
SHOW YOUR WORK

1. Makoto, Sam, Julia, and Terrell are all cousins. Makoto is 3 years older than Sam. Sam is 2 years older than Julia. Julia is 2 years older than Terrell. Terrell is 5 years old. How old is Makoto?

   Makoto is _____ years old.

2. On a math quiz, Michelle scored 7 points higher than Darnell. Darnell scored 3 points higher than Andrea. Andrea scored 1 point higher than Frankie. Frankie scored 81 points on the math quiz. What was Michelle's score on the math quiz?

   Michelle scored a _____ on the math quiz.

3. Daniella stopped by a convenience store and bought 2 L of milk that cost $3.79 and a bag of chips that cost $2.24. The cashier gave her $3.97 back in change. How much money did Daniella give the cashier to pay for the milk and chips?

   Daniella gave the cashier _____ to pay for the milk and chips.

PROBLEM-SOLVING STRATEGIES
Estimation

Mrs. Whitmer stopped by the meat market to buy some meat for dinner. She wants to buy pork chops and roast. The pork chops cost $1.79 each and the roast costs $3.89 per kilogram.

She needs to buy 5 pork chops and a 3 kg of roast. About how much will she spend on the meat?

Use estimation to find the cost of each type of meat.

Mrs. Whitmer will spend about __$22.00__ .

Since the pork chops cost $1.79 each, round to $2.00 each and multiply by 5.

$$\begin{array}{r} \$2.00 \\ \times 5 \\ \hline \$10.00 \end{array}$$

Since the roast costs $3.89 per kilogram, round to $4.00 per kilogram and multiply by 3.

$$\begin{array}{r} \$4.00 \\ \times 3 \\ \hline \$12.00 \end{array}$$

$$\$10.00 + \$12.00 = \$22.00$$

Solve each problem.

SHOW YOUR WORK

1. At the bookstore, Josh wants to buy two magazines that cost $3.75 each and a book that costs $6.12. About how much will it cost for these three items?

   It will cost about _____.

---

2. On Monday, 769 people visited the museum. On Tuesday, 524 people visited the museum. On Wednesday, 580 people visited the museum. About how many people visited the museum on Monday, Tuesday, and Wednesday?

   About _____ people visited the museum.

---

3. For lunch, Bret is either going to buy soup and salad or a sandwich and chips. The soup is $1.79, a salad is $3.15, a sandwich is $4.95, and chips are $0.89. Which meal would be less expensive: soup and salad or sandwich and chips?

   _____ would be a less expensive lunch.

CHAPTER 1   PRETEST
Addition and Subtraction (2-digit through 5-digit)

Add or subtract.

	a	b	c	d	e
1.	4 2 +2 6	3 7 +4 8	2 3 +9 5	7 6 +4 8	4 8 +3 9
2.	8 4 −2 3	7 5 −2 6	1 7 3 −9 2	1 6 5 −8 7	1 0 8 −3 9
3.	4 2 1 +3 5 7	8 3 2 +1 4 9	2 6 7 +1 3 8	5 2 1 +7 8 3	9 5 6 +2 8 7
4.	8 5 4 −3 2 1	7 8 3 −6 2 5	9 2 1 −5 7 0	1 4 3 6 −3 4 9	1 7 9 3 −8 7 5
5.	4 2 3 5 +3 7 9 6	6 5 1 8 +4 7 3 9	5 1 6 7 2 +4 3 1 8	5 2 1 9 6 +3 8 4 1 7	2 5 1 8 6 +3 5 8 2 1
6.	7 6 5 9 −3 8 4 7	8 2 5 0 −6 3 7 4	5 2 1 6 9 −3 0 5 7	4 2 1 9 6 −3 8 4 2 7	5 2 1 0 5 −3 8 1 5 6
7.	4 2 5 7 +3 8	3 4 2 7 +8 6	3 7 5 2 4 6 +3 8 1	6 0 2 3 4 0 3 4 +7 0 1 2	7 3 1 5 2 4 3 0 8 1 +5 2 1 6 5
8.	5 4 2 7 3 8 +4 6	7 3 1 2 0 8 3 1 9 +4 2 6	5 0 0 3 6 4 2 1 7 3 9 0 +3 2 4	8 2 1 6 4 3 1 5 2 1 7 3 4 0 8 1 +5 2 1 6	7 0 8 1 2 3 2 1 8 1 3 1 2 1 8 6 1 4 0 8 +3 0 8 0 2

MacDonald 33 Clark 24
Time 3:01
Quarter 3

Solve each problem.

1. How many points have been scored by both teams?

MacDonald has scored _____ points.

Clark has scored _____ points.

Both teams have scored _____ points.

2. Which team is ahead? By how many points are they ahead?

_____ is ahead.

They are ahead by _____ points.

3. During the rest of the game MacDonald scored 10 more points and Clark scored 12 more points. Which team won the game? By how many points did they win?

The final score for MacDonald was _____.

The final score for Clark was _____.

_____ won the game.

They won by _____ points.

1.

2.

3.

Lesson 3 Addition and Subtraction (2- and 3-digit)

Add the ones.
Rename.

Add the tens.

Rename 146 as "1 hundred, 3 tens, and 16 ones." Then subtract the ones.

Rename 1 hundred and 3 tens as "13 tens." Then subtract the tens.

```
        8       58      58     146        3 16         13
 58    +9      +89     +89    −87       1 4 6        1 4 6
+89    1 7      7      147            − 8 7        − 8 7
                                          9          5 9
```

Add.

	a	b	c	d	e	f
1.	23 +54	63 +25	72 +16	43 +54	26 +31	27 +42
2.	27 +35	47 +28	65 +26	31 +49	56 +28	39 +26
3.	47 +78	57 +86	32 +79	67 +84	36 +96	56 +47
4.	36 +27	45 +23	77 +77	63 +42	56 +24	35 +75

Subtract.

	a	b	c	d	e	f
5.	76 −24	37 −22	89 −63	75 −24	65 −31	49 −30
6.	95 −26	38 −19	52 −27	65 −48	91 −73	54 −27
7.	126 −37	143 −95	156 −88	172 −76	168 −99	153 −85

Lesson 3 Problem Solving

Solve each problem.

1. Sarah's father worked 36 h one week and 47 h the next week. How many hours did he work during these two weeks?

   He worked _____ h the first week.

   He worked _____ h the second week.

   During these 2 weeks, he worked a total of _____ h.

   1.

2. Seventy-six people live in Logan's apartment building. In Mike's apartment building, there are 85 people. How many more people live in Mike's building than in Logan's building?

   _____ people live in Mike's building.

   _____ people live in Logan's building.

   _____ more people live in Mike's building.

   2.

3. In problem **2,** how many people live in both Logan's and Mike's apartment buildings?

   _____ people live in both buildings.

   3.

4. There are 103 pages in Vera's new book. She has read 35 pages. How many pages does she have left to read?

   There are _____ pages in the book.

   She has read _____ pages.

   She has _____ pages left to read.

   4.

5. Paula lives 53 km from Dartmouth. Ann lives 85 km from Dartmouth. How many kilometres closer to Dartmouth does Paula live than Ann?

   Paula lives _____ km closer.

   5.

Lesson 4   Addition and Subtraction
(3- and 4-digit)

Add from right to left.

$$
\begin{array}{r} ^{1}\ \\ 754 \\ +587 \\ \hline 1 \end{array}
\qquad
\begin{array}{r} ^{1}\ ^{1} \\ 754 \\ +587 \\ \hline 41 \end{array}
\qquad
\begin{array}{r} ^{1}\ ^{1} \\ 754 \\ +587 \\ \hline 1341 \end{array}
$$

Subtract from right to left.

$$
\begin{array}{r} ^{3\ 11} \\ 134\!\!\!/1 \\ -587 \\ \hline 4 \end{array}
\qquad
\begin{array}{r} ^{13} \\ ^{2\ 3\ 11} \\ 1\!\!\!/3\!\!\!/4\!\!\!/1 \\ -587 \\ \hline 54 \end{array}
\qquad
\begin{array}{r} ^{12\ 13} \\ ^{2\ 3\ 11} \\ 1\!\!\!/3\!\!\!/4\!\!\!/1 \\ -587 \\ \hline 754 \end{array}
$$

Add.

	a	b	c	d	e	f
1.	$\begin{array}{r}314\\+482\end{array}$	$\begin{array}{r}703\\+192\end{array}$	$\begin{array}{r}542\\+318\end{array}$	$\begin{array}{r}265\\+429\end{array}$	$\begin{array}{r}553\\+274\end{array}$	$\begin{array}{r}629\\+280\end{array}$
2.	$\begin{array}{r}483\\+702\end{array}$	$\begin{array}{r}546\\+931\end{array}$	$\begin{array}{r}736\\+279\end{array}$	$\begin{array}{r}653\\+199\end{array}$	$\begin{array}{r}706\\+539\end{array}$	$\begin{array}{r}582\\+609\end{array}$
3.	$\begin{array}{r}813\\+792\end{array}$	$\begin{array}{r}763\\+762\end{array}$	$\begin{array}{r}423\\+798\end{array}$	$\begin{array}{r}358\\+759\end{array}$	$\begin{array}{r}816\\+395\end{array}$	$\begin{array}{r}926\\+178\end{array}$

Subtract.

	a	b	c	d	e	f
4.	$\begin{array}{r}784\\-362\end{array}$	$\begin{array}{r}927\\-405\end{array}$	$\begin{array}{r}542\\-314\end{array}$	$\begin{array}{r}765\\-238\end{array}$	$\begin{array}{r}926\\-341\end{array}$	$\begin{array}{r}563\\-281\end{array}$
5.	$\begin{array}{r}1732\\-812\end{array}$	$\begin{array}{r}1574\\-923\end{array}$	$\begin{array}{r}1764\\-925\end{array}$	$\begin{array}{r}1345\\-629\end{array}$	$\begin{array}{r}1542\\-286\end{array}$	$\begin{array}{r}1637\\-439\end{array}$
6.	$\begin{array}{r}1563\\-678\end{array}$	$\begin{array}{r}1322\\-733\end{array}$	$\begin{array}{r}1580\\-687\end{array}$	$\begin{array}{r}1629\\-243\end{array}$	$\begin{array}{r}1435\\-162\end{array}$	$\begin{array}{r}1748\\-358\end{array}$
7.	$\begin{array}{r}1984\\-362\end{array}$	$\begin{array}{r}1864\\-372\end{array}$	$\begin{array}{r}1250\\-741\end{array}$	$\begin{array}{r}1608\\-413\end{array}$	$\begin{array}{r}1500\\-263\end{array}$	$\begin{array}{r}1542\\-245\end{array}$

Lesson 4 Problem Solving

Answer each question.

1. The odometer reading on Mrs. Lee's car is 142. On
   Mr. Cook's, it is 319. How many more kilometres
   does Mr. Cook have on his car than Mrs. Lee?

   Are you to add
      or subtract? _____

   How many more kilometres does Mr. Cook have
      on his car than Mrs. Lee? _____

   1.

2. Carmen and Ava collect trading stamps. Carmen
   has 423 trading stamps and Ava has 519. How
   many stamps do both girls have?

   Are you to add
      or subtract? _____

   How many stamps
      do both girls have? _____

   2.

3. Helen's family drove 975 km on their vacation
   last year and 776 km this year. How many
   kilometres did they travel during these two
   vacations?

   Are you to add
      or subtract? _____

   How many kilometres did they travel
      during these two vacations? _____

   3.

4. In problem **3**, how many more kilometres did they
   travel during the first year than the last?

   Are you to add
      or subtract? _____

   How many more kilometres did they travel during
      the first year than the last? _____

   4.

5. Tricia needs 293 more points to win a prize. It
   takes 1500 points to win a prize. How many points
   does Tricia have now?

   Are you to add
      or subtract? _____

   How many points
      does she have now? _____

   5.

Lesson 5 Addition and Subtraction
(4- and 5-digit)

Add.	21 345	Subtract.	30 807
	+9 462		−9 462
	30 807		21 345
Check.	−9 462	Check.	+9 462
	21 345		30 807

These should be the same.

These should be the same.

Add. Check each answer.

	a	b	c
1.	3 0 8 2 1 +4 1 6 3	5 2 9 6 4 +3 1 7 5	7 6 4 8 7 +5 2 4 3
2.	4 2 5 6 3 +1 5 7 8 6	1 5 2 4 3 +2 7 5 6 1	3 6 7 2 4 +8 1 4 0 9

Subtract. Check each answer.

3.	7 2 4 3 1 −5 3 1 6	9 2 6 4 0 −6 7 4 1	6 1 4 3 0 −6 4 2 9
4.	5 4 0 6 1 −6 8 3 5	7 2 4 1 3 −6 7 8 5	8 4 2 0 5 −5 1 1 6

Lesson 5 Problem Solving

Solve each problem. Check each answer.

1. The space flight is expected to last 11 720 min. They are now 7342 min into the flight. How many minutes remain?

   _____ min remain in the flight.

   1.

2. In one year Mrs. Ching drove the company car 13 428 km and her personal car 8489 km. How many kilometres did she drive both cars?

   She drove _____ km.

   2.

3. In problem **2**, how many fewer kilometres did she drive her personal car than the company car?

   She drove her personal car _____ km fewer.

   3.

4. The factory where Mr. Whitmal works produced 3173 fewer parts this month than last. The factory produced 42 916 parts this month. How many parts did it produce last month?

   The factory produced _____ parts last month.

   4.

5. Suppose the factory in problem **4** produced 3173 more parts this month than last. How many parts would it have produced last month?

   _____ parts would have been produced.

   5.

6. There are 86 400 s in a day. How many seconds are there in 2 days?

   There are _____ s in two days.

   6.

7. During one month Joanne spent 14 400 min sleeping and 5800 min eating. How much total time did she spend eating and sleeping?

   She spent _____ min eating and sleeping.

   7.

Lesson 6   Addition (3 or more numbers)

Add the ones.

```
  3675          5      3675          Follow the same       1 12
  1406          6      1406          pattern to add        3 675
  3759          9      3759          the tens, the         1 406
 +6134         +4     +6134          hundreds, and         3 759
              ② 4        4           so on.               +6 134
                                                          14 974
```

Add.

	a	b	c	d	e

1.

```
    4 5 3        2 3 1        2 4 2        7 2 6        5 4 2
    2 1 6        4 2 5        3 7 5        6 3 0        4 1 6
   +3 2 0       +3 1 7       +1 6 1       +7 1 2       +5 3 7
```

2.

```
  6 3 1 4      2 1 6 5      8 0 9 3    7 2 1 9 3    7 2 1 6 5
  2 1 4 5      3 4 2 0      1 2 4 6    8 3 4 7 0    4 5 2 3 0
 +7 6 3 4     +7 0 1 5      +5 4 3   +2 1 6 5 9    +3 2 1 6
```

3.

```
    3 2 5        7 2 6      7 3 1 6      8 2 1 6    9 2 1 6 3
    4 6 3        3 1 4      1 4 2 5      7 3 4 3    4 8 5 1 7
    1 7 9        5 4 0      7 8 3 4    8 1 6 9 2    7 3 2 1 4
   +2 5 8       +8 2 9     +2 4 0 1   +4 0 8 3 0   +8 2 1 1 9
```

4.

```
    7 3 0      3 8 2 9      8 2 1 3    3 6 0 0 0    4 2 1 6 5
    4 6 0      1 3 6 4      4 1 0 6    7 2 4 5 0    3 0 7 0 8
    2 7 3      1 2 7 4      2 3 0 0    8 3 1 9 2    2 9 1 1 5
    8 9 2        4 2 9      4 8 1 9    6 2 4 5 1    4 0 0 8 2
   +4 5 3       +6 7 0     +2 7 4 5   +3 1 9 2 4   +3 1 6 2 1
```

5.

```
    5 4 2      1 6 2 8      4 2 1 6    5 2 1 6 3        3 1 6
    3 6 5        3 2 9    5 3 0 0 8      4 2 1 8      2 1 4 3
    4 2 1      1 7 5 4    4 2 1 3 4        3 1 6        1 2 6
    3 0 0        3 2 1      2 1 6 5      5 4 2 1    5 2 1 4 0
    4 6 0        6 0 8      3 0 0 8    6 2 1 9 0      1 2 3 0
   +5 2 3     +2 9 1 1    +4 0 0 0      +4 2 0       +6 8 0
```

Lesson 6   Problem Solving

Solve each problem.

1. During the summer reading program, Faye read 752 pages. Barbara read 436 pages. Cameron read 521 pages. How many pages did these students read in all?

   They read _____ pages in all.

2. During September Joe travelled the following numbers of kilometres: 421, 308, 240, and 571. What was the total number of kilometres he travelled?

   He travelled a total of _____ km.

3. Four astronauts have logged the following times in actual space travel: 4216 min, 14 628 min, 3153 min, and 22 117 min. How many minutes have all four astronauts logged in actual space travel?

   All four have logged _____ min in space.

4. The numbers of parts shipped to six cities were as follows: 317, 2410, 32 415, 4068, 321, and 5218. How many parts were shipped in all?

   _____ parts were shipped.

5. A recent census gave the following populations: Adel, 4321; Alcroft, 55 890; Alma, 3515; Alto Park, 2526; Amherst, 13 472; and Ashburn, 3291. What is the total population of these places?

   The total population is _____.

6. In an earlier census, the populations of the towns listed in problem 5 were 2776, 31 155, 2588, 1195, 11 389, and 2918, respectively. What was the total population then?

   Then the total population was _____.

7. In problem 5, what is the total population of Adel, Alcroft, and Alto Park?

   The total population is _____.

1.

2.

3.

4.

5.

6.

7.

Lesson 7   Estimating Sums and Differences

Round each number to the highest place value the numbers have in common. Then add from right to left.

$$
\begin{array}{r}
382 \longrightarrow 400 \\
+733 \longrightarrow +700 \\
\hline
1100
\end{array}
$$

Round each number to the highest place value they have in common. Then subtract from right to left.

$$
\begin{array}{r}
27\ 125 \longrightarrow 27\ 000 \\
-8\ 734 \longrightarrow -9\ 000 \\
\hline
18\ 000
\end{array}
$$

Estimate each sum or difference.

	a	b	c	d	e
1.	6 8 +3 4	2 7 +8 1	2 9 +3 6	9 3 +4 5	1 7 4 +8 8
2.	4 7 −2 6	9 4 −5 8	6 6 −5 7	8 2 −3 4	3 7 3 −8 9
3.	4 8 3 +2 3 7	6 6 8 +3 1 9	2 7 1 +9 2 6	2 3 2 5 +7 6 0	8 2 7 +9 5 8
4.	7 2 3 −2 8 5	5 4 3 −1 6 4	2 3 9 −1 2 4	6 7 8 −1 3 5	2 9 2 3 −1 7 6 5
5.	4 1 6 5 +7 5 8 4	1 2 1 9 +3 4 7 0	9 8 4 3 +5 1 9 4	3 2 6 2 1 +8 3 1 9	2 2 4 7 3 +1 5 7 0 4
6.	9 2 6 1 −3 4 2 5	8 4 9 8 −2 7 5 7	9 0 3 2 −3 9 4 0	4 5 4 6 2 −2 4 3 1 8	1 3 8 5 2 −9 4 6 5
7.	5 6 1 8 0 7 +5 3 4	3 6 1 5 8 1 2 4 +4 3 1 9	9 2 7 3 1 2 4 0 5 +6 7 9 3	2 9 6 1 8 9 1 1 2 8 +7 3 5 8 4	1 0 7 3 7 4 4 2 9 8 1 +6 4 5 6 3

Lesson 7　Problem Solving

Solve each problem. Use estimation.

1. On Monday, Carlos drove 273 km. On Tuesday, he drove 129 km. About how many more kilometres did Carlos drive on Monday than on Tuesday?

Are you to add or subtract? _____

Carlos drove about _____ km more?

1.

2. Deena and Kayla both keep all their coins in a jar. Deena has 83 coins in her jar and Kayla has 76 coins in her jar. Together, about how many coins do Deena and Kayla have in their jars?

Are you to add or subtract? _____

Deena and Kayla have about _____ coins.

2.

3. At the arcade you get tickets by winning at several different games. After a year, Malcom had saved 2391 tickets and Brent had saved 3608 tickets. If Malcolm and Brent combine their tickets to get one big prize, about how many tickets would they have?

Are you to add or subtract? _____

Malcolm and Brent have about _____ tickets.

3.

4. The Oakdale School auditorium holds 3285 people. The Oakdale School gymnasium holds 1340 people. About how many more people does the auditorium hold than the gymnasium?

Are you to add or subtract? _____

The auditorium holds about _____ more people.

4.

5. Monica kept track of the number of pages she read each month over the summer. In June she read 319 pages. In July she read 185 pages. In August she read 227 pages. About how many pages did Monica read during the summer months?

Are you to add or subtract? _____

Monica read about _____ pages.

5.

CHAPTER 1   PRACTICE TEST
Addition and Subtraction (2-digit through 5-digit)

Add or subtract.

	a	*b*	*c*	*d*	*e*
1.	46 +32	423 +268	1829 +3573	7521 +3609	52 163 +72 845
2.	85 −32	564 −382	1936 −479	18 312 −9 264	10 306 −2 568
3.	32 26 +13	724 380 +465	295 327 168 +269	5534 1468 3137 +2950	42 163 30 820 21 911 +60 422
4.	7832 −1467	8309 −2654	13 182 −4 296	91 234 −82 169	72 085 −36 526

Solve each problem.

5. The following points were earned in a ticket-selling contest: Ashley, 2320; Taylor, 1564; Ali, 907; Lyn, 852; Marty, 775. What was the total number of points earned by Ashley and Ali?

Ashley earned _____ points.

Ali earned _____ points.

They earned a total of _____ points.

5.

6. In problem **5**, what was the total number of points earned by all five students?

They earned a total of _____ points.

6.

7. In problem **5**, how many more points did Taylor earn than Marty?

Taylor earned _____ more points.

7.

CHAPTER 2 PRETEST
Multiplication (2-digit by 1-digit through 4-digit by 3-digit)

Multiply.

	a	*b*	*c*	*d*
1.	24 ×2	35 ×2	154 ×6	678 ×9
2.	31 ×23	82 ×18	45 ×51	87 ×39
3.	143 ×22	734 ×19	253 ×62	708 ×36
4.	321 ×123	432 ×621	507 ×143	821 ×105
5.	3126 ×422	4032 ×145	3124 ×712	8197 ×325

Lesson 1 Multiplication Facts

Multiply.

	a	*b*	*c*	*d*	*e*	*f*	*g*	*h*
1.	4 ×2	8 ×2	7 ×2	2 ×2	6 ×2	5 ×2	3 ×2	1 ×2
2.	8 ×3	2 ×3	9 ×3	6 ×3	5 ×3	0 ×3	4 ×3	3 ×3
3.	2 ×4	1 ×4	6 ×4	8 ×4	7 ×4	3 ×4	9 ×4	4 ×4
4.	7 ×5	5 ×5	2 ×5	6 ×5	4 ×5	9 ×5	3 ×5	8 ×5
5.	6 ×6	2 ×6	9 ×6	3 ×6	1 ×6	7 ×6	5 ×6	8 ×6
6.	1 ×7	3 ×7	9 ×7	2 ×7	6 ×7	7 ×7	8 ×7	5 ×7
7.	5 ×8	1 ×8	7 ×8	2 ×8	9 ×8	6 ×8	3 ×8	8 ×8
8.	8 ×9	2 ×9	1 ×9	6 ×9	7 ×9	4 ×9	5 ×9	9 ×9
9.	3 ×0	8 ×0	0 ×0	1 ×0	6 ×1	2 ×1	9 ×1	7 ×1

CHAPTER 2

Lesson 1 Problem Solving

Solve each problem.

1. There are six rows of desks in the classroom. Each row has eight desks. How many desks are in the classroom?

There are _____ rows of desks.

There are _____ desks in each row.

There are _____ desks in all.

1.

2. There are nine rows of trees. There are seven trees in each row. How many trees are there in all?

There are _____ rows of trees.

There are _____ trees in each row.

There are _____ trees in all.

2.

3. The people at the park were separated into teams of eight people each. Nine teams were formed. How many people were in the park?

Each team had _____ people.

There were _____ teams formed.

There were _____ people in the park.

3.

4. There are six people in each car. There were seven cars. How many people were there in all?

There were _____ people in each car.

There were _____ cars.

There were _____ people in all.

4.

5. How many cents would you need to buy eight 8-cent pencils?

You would need _____ cents.

5.   **6.**

6. There are five oranges in each sack. How many oranges would there be in nine sacks?

There would be _____ oranges in nine sacks.

Lesson 2 Multiplication (by 1-digit)

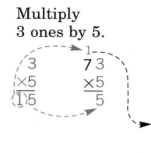

Multiply
3 ones by 5.

Multiply 7 tens by 5.
Add the tens.

```
  1
3     73
×5    ×5
15     5
```

```
  7  tens      73
  ×5            ×5
  35  tens     365
  +1  ten
  36  tens
```

```
   2
 327
  ×4
   8
```

```
  1 2
 327
  ×4
  08
```

```
  1 2
 327
  ×4
 1308
```

Multiply.

	a	b	c	d	e	f
1.	3 2 ×2	2 1 ×3	4 2 ×2	1 3 2 ×2	2 1 3 ×3	4 2 1 ×2
2.	1 6 ×4	3 6 ×2	2 8 ×3	1 2 3 ×4	1 2 7 ×3	2 1 5 ×4
3.	7 3 ×3	4 2 ×4	8 1 ×5	3 5 2 ×2	1 7 2 ×4	2 6 3 ×3
4.	5 7 ×5	2 8 ×6	3 7 ×4	2 5 6 ×3	3 8 5 ×2	1 7 7 ×5
5.	2 8 ×6	4 7 ×8	3 9 ×5	4 2 6 ×7	3 5 8 ×6	2 3 4 ×5
6.	5 7 ×8	4 8 ×2	7 0 ×5	5 2 6 ×3	4 0 9 ×5	7 3 0 ×7
7.	7 2 ×9	9 5 ×7	8 1 ×8	6 2 9 ×8	8 0 1 ×7	6 5 8 ×9

Lesson 2 Problem Solving

Solve each problem.

1. Each club member works 3 h each month. There
   are 32 members. What is the total number of hours
   worked each month by all club members?

   There are _____ club members.

   Each member works _____ h.

   The club members work _____ h in all.

1.

2. Mrs. Robins drives 19 km every working day.
   How many kilometres does she drive in a 5-day
   workweek?

   She drives _____ km every working day.

   She works _____ days a week.

   She drives _____ km in a 5-day workweek.

2.

3. It takes 54 min to make one pillow. How long will
   it take to make 3 pillows?

   It takes _____ min to make one pillow.

   There are _____ pillows.

   It takes _____ min to make 3 pillows.

3.

4. Each box has a mass of 121 kg. There are four
   boxes. What is the total mass of the four boxes?

   Each box has a mass of _____ kg.

   There are _____ boxes.

   The total mass of the four boxes is _____ kg.

4.

5. There are 168 h in a week. How many hours are
   there in 6 weeks?

   There are _____ h in 6 weeks.

5.

6.

6. There were 708 employees at work today. Each
   employee worked 8 h. How many hours did these
   employees work?

   _____ h were worked.

Lesson 3   Multiplication (by 2-digit)

```
  41       41       56       56
  ×2      ×20       ×3      ×30
  82      820      168     1680
```

If $2 \times 41 = 82$, then $20 \times 41 =$ _____.

If $3 \times 56 = 168$, then $30 \times 56 =$ _____.

If $4 \times 27 = 108$, then $40 \times 27 =$ _____.

Multiply 56 by 1.	Multiply 56 by 30.

```
   56        56          56
  ×31       ×31         ×31
   56        56          56 ⎫
            1680       1680 ⎭ Add.
                       1736
```

Multiply.

	a	b	c	d	e	f
1.	2 3 ×3	2 3 ×3 0	4 3 ×2	4 3 ×2 0	5 1 ×4	5 1 ×4 0
2.	3 7 ×4	3 7 ×4 0	5 4 ×6	5 4 ×6 0	7 3 ×9	7 3 ×9 0
2.	4 2 ×3 0	7 5 ×2 0	5 4 ×4 0	6 2 ×7 0	8 4 ×6 0	3 2 ×5 0

Multiply.

	a	b	c	d	e
4.	3 1 ×2 3	4 2 ×3 3	4 5 ×1 2	1 7 ×3 5	3 6 ×2 4
5.	5 4 ×2 6	3 7 ×4 1	2 8 ×1 6	3 8 ×7 3	4 6 ×2 8

Lesson 3 Problem Solving

Solve each problem.

1. There are 60 min in 1 h. How many minutes are there in 24 h?

   There are _____ min in 24 h.

2. Forty-eight toy boats are packed in each box. How many boats are there in 16 boxes?

   There are _____ boats in 16 boxes.

3. Seventy-three new cars can be assembled in 1 h. At that rate, how many cars could be assembled in 51 h?

   _____ cars could be assembled in 51 h.

4. A truck is hauling 36 bags of cement. Each bag has a mass of 42 kg. How many kilograms of cement are being hauled?

   _____ kg of cement are being hauled.

5. To square a number means to multiply the number by itself. What is the square of 68?

   The square of 68 is _____.

6. Sixty-five books are packed in each box. How many books are there in 85 boxes?

   There are _____ books in 85 boxes.

7. Every classroom in Jan's school has at least 29 desks. There are 38 classrooms in all. What is the least number of desks in the school?

   There are at least _____ desks.

8. Some students came to the museum on 12 buses. There were 58 students on each bus. How many students came to the museum by bus?

   _____ students came by bus.

1.	2.
3.	4.
5.	6.
7.	8.

Lesson 4 Multiplication (by 2-digit)

	Multiply 351 by 7.	**Multiply** 351 by 20.	
351 ×27	351 ×27 2457	351 ×27 2457 7020	351 ×27 2457 } Add. 7020 } 9477

Multiply.

	a	*b*	*c*	*d*	*e*
1.	4 2 ×1 3	2 3 ×3 2	5 4 ×4 1	3 7 ×2 6	5 8 ×1 9
2.	5 8 ×7 2	2 7 ×3 6	4 0 ×5 5	2 7 ×2 7	3 9 ×4 2
3.	1 5 4 ×1 3	2 3 1 ×2 6	2 5 1 ×4 1	3 1 2 ×3 2	4 1 5 ×4 7
4.	3 6 5 ×2 7	4 2 6 ×1 3	7 1 5 ×2 6	3 0 2 ×4 3	7 5 6 ×2 9

Lesson 4 Problem Solving

Solve each problem.

1. A machine can produce 98 parts in 1 h. How many parts could it produce in 72 h?

It could produce _____ parts in 72 h.

2. Each new bus can carry 66 passengers. How many passengers can ride on 85 new buses?

_____ passengers can ride on 85 buses.

3. How many hours are there in a year (365 days)?

There are _____ h in a year.

4. Each of 583 people worked a 40-h week. How many hours of work was this?

It was _____ h of work.

5. The highway distance between Toronto and Montréal is 545 km. How many kilometres would a bus travel in making 68 one-way trips between Toronto and Montréal?

The bus would travel _____ km.

6. The flying distance between the cities in problem **5** is 439 km. What is the least number of kilometres a plane would travel in making 57 one-way trips?

The least number of kilometres would be _____.

7. The rail distance between Halifax and Montréal is 1346 km. How many kilometres would a train travel in making 52 one-way trips?

It would travel _____ km.

8. The airline distance between the cities in problem **7** is 924 km. What is the least number of kilometres a plane would travel in making 45 one-way trips?

The least number of kilometres would be _____.

1.	2.
3.	4.
5.	6.
7.	8.

Lesson 5 Multiplication (by 3-digit)

```
  3254            3 254            3 254     | 3 254
   ×2              ×20             ×200      | ×213
  6508            65 080          650 800    | 9 762 ———————3×3254
                                            | 32 540 ——————10×3254
                                            | 650 800 ————— 200×3254
If 2 × 3254 = 6508, then 20 × 3254 = _____.    | 693 102    Add.

If 2 × 3254 = 6508, then 200 × 3254 = _____.
```

Multiply.

	a	*b*	*c*	*d*

1.
```
   3 1 6          3 1 6          4 2 8 1        4 2 8 1
    ×2           ×2 0 0            ×3           ×3 0 0
```

2.
```
   4 1 6          3 7 5          4 0 8          2 1 9
 ×2 1 3          ×2 9 1         ×3 1 6         ×5 0 3
```

3.
```
   3 1 6          4 8 3          4 2 3 1        3 4 5 6
 ×2 7 5          ×2 1 1         ×2 1 3         ×1 2 3
```

4.
```
  2 1 7 5         3 2 1 6        3 0 9 0        6 6 1 3
  ×2 4 3          ×2 0 8         ×7 5 2         ×3 4 2
```

Lesson 5 Problem Solving

Solve each problem.

1. Each crate unloaded had a mass of 342 kg. 212 crates were unloaded. How many kilograms were unloaded?

   _____ kg were unloaded.

2. The school cafeteria expects to serve 425 customers every day. At that rate, how many meals will be served if the cafeteria is open 175 days a year?

   _____ meals will be served.

3. There are 168 h in one week. How many hours are there in 260 weeks?

   There are _____ h in 260 weeks.

4. There are 3600 s in 1 h and 168 h in 1 week. How many seconds are there in 1 week?

   There are _____ s in 1 week.

5. A jet carrying 128 passengers flew 2574 km. How many passenger-kilometres (number of passengers times number of kilometres travelled) did it fly?

   It flew _____ passenger-kilometres.

6. How many passenger-kilometres would be flown by the jet in problem 5 if it flew a distance of 2098 km?

   It would be _____ passenger-kilometres.

7. A tanker truck made 275 trips in a year. It hauled 11 500 L each trip. How many litres did it haul that year?

   It hauled _____ L.

8. Suppose the truck in problem 7 hauled 22 700 L each trip. How many litres would it haul?

   It would haul _____ L.

1.	2.
3.	4.
5.	6.
7.	8.

Lesson 6 Estimating Products

Round 68 to 70. Then multiply from right to left.

$$68 \longrightarrow 70$$
$$\times 3 \qquad \times 3$$
$$\overline{210}$$

Round each number to its highest place value.

$$625 \longrightarrow 600$$
$$\times 381 \longrightarrow \times 400$$
$$\overline{240\ 000}$$

Estimate each product.

	a	b	c	d	e
1.	84 ×7	43 ×6	87 ×3	66 ×9	91 ×5
2.	384 ×4	618 ×9	382 ×7	633 ×2	908 ×8
3.	28 ×37	39 ×75	76 ×18	48 ×37	63 ×47
4.	943 ×56	249 ×33	164 ×55	116 ×89	649 ×35
5.	329 ×607	261 ×329	892 ×219	740 ×273	819 ×464
6.	1862 ×97	6208 ×73	4935 ×48	1206 ×67	3496 ×13
7.	9815 ×264	4806 ×492	5930 ×228	2608 ×691	7393 ×535

Lesson 6 Problem Solving

Solve each problem. Use estimation.

1. Tyron read 18 pages each night for 1 week. About how many pages did he read that week?

   Tyron read about _____ pages that week.

2. One type of airplane can carry up to 118 passengers. About how many passengers can five such airplanes carry?

   Five such airplanes can carry about _____ passengers.

3. Kim watched three movies one weekend that were 96 min each. About how many minutes did Kim spend watching movies?

   Kim spent about _____ min watching movies one weekend.

4. Alan has a paper route. He delivers 22 newspapers each hour. If it takes him 4 h to deliver all the newspapers in his route, about how many newspapers does he deliver?

   Alan delivers about _____ newspapers on his paper route.

5. A machine produces 367 gadgets in 1 h. Each day the machine continually runs for 18 h. About how many gadgets does the machine produce in 1 day?

   The machine produces about _____ gadgets in 1 day.

6. Jasmine is on the cross-country team. Each day the team practises, the team members run 5 km. If the team will have 32 practices this season, about how many kilometres will Jasmine run at practice this season?

   Jasmine will run about _____ km at practice this season.

1.

2.

3.

4.

5.

6.

CHAPTER 2   PRACTICE TEST
Multiplication (2-digit by 1-digit through 4-digit by 3-digit)

Multiply.

	a	*b*	*c*	*d*
1.	$\begin{array}{r} 31 \\ \times 3 \\ \hline \end{array}$	$\begin{array}{r} 25 \\ \times 3 \\ \hline \end{array}$	$\begin{array}{r} 276 \\ \times 6 \\ \hline \end{array}$	$\begin{array}{r} 583 \\ \times 7 \\ \hline \end{array}$
2.	$\begin{array}{r} 23 \\ \times 13 \\ \hline \end{array}$	$\begin{array}{r} 42 \\ \times 26 \\ \hline \end{array}$	$\begin{array}{r} 38 \\ \times 17 \\ \hline \end{array}$	$\begin{array}{r} 53 \\ \times 45 \\ \hline \end{array}$
3.	$\begin{array}{r} 123 \\ \times 31 \\ \hline \end{array}$	$\begin{array}{r} 425 \\ \times 70 \\ \hline \end{array}$	$\begin{array}{r} 563 \\ \times 25 \\ \hline \end{array}$	$\begin{array}{r} 837 \\ \times 85 \\ \hline \end{array}$
4.	$\begin{array}{r} 213 \\ \times 132 \\ \hline \end{array}$	$\begin{array}{r} 421 \\ \times 378 \\ \hline \end{array}$	$\begin{array}{r} 256 \\ \times 108 \\ \hline \end{array}$	$\begin{array}{r} 845 \\ \times 374 \\ \hline \end{array}$
5.	$\begin{array}{r} 1221 \\ \times 312 \\ \hline \end{array}$	$\begin{array}{r} 1456 \\ \times 173 \\ \hline \end{array}$	$\begin{array}{r} 1827 \\ \times 570 \\ \hline \end{array}$	$\begin{array}{r} 3456 \\ \times 732 \\ \hline \end{array}$

CHAPTER 3   PRETEST
Division (2-digit through 4-digit by 1-digit)

Divide.

	a	*b*	*c*	*d*
1.	$7\overline{)63}$	$6\overline{)54}$	$5\overline{)75}$	$4\overline{)92}$
2.	$4\overline{)136}$	$5\overline{)370}$	$3\overline{)471}$	$2\overline{)960}$
3.	$3\overline{)1539}$	$4\overline{)3672}$	$7\overline{)7105}$	$5\overline{)8605}$
4.	$4\overline{)87}$	$2\overline{)75}$	$3\overline{)86}$	$3\overline{)781}$
5.	$6\overline{)143}$	$4\overline{)9226}$	$2\overline{)1435}$	$5\overline{)6134}$

Lesson 1   Division Facts

If $5 \times 9 = 45$, then $45 \div 5 = 9$ and $45 \div 9 = 5$.

Divide.

	a	b	c	d	e	f
1.	2)‾6	3)‾9	2)‾4	2)‾8	3)‾6	4)‾8
2.	1)‾5	3)‾3	6)‾0	1)‾9	2)‾2	7)‾7
3.	4)‾28	6)‾42	3)‾18	6)‾36	8)‾32	2)‾14
4.	2)‾10	8)‾72	7)‾42	5)‾20	3)‾15	4)‾36
5.	8)‾24	2)‾18	1)‾8	4)‾32	5)‾25	9)‾81
6.	7)‾35	9)‾27	6)‾24	7)‾49	8)‾48	9)‾36
7.	5)‾40	3)‾24	2)‾16	6)‾48	7)‾28	9)‾54
8.	5)‾15	4)‾12	2)‾12	3)‾0	6)‾54	3)‾27
9.	4)‾20	8)‾56	6)‾30	4)‾24	3)‾21	5)‾30
10.	8)‾16	5)‾35	4)‾16	8)‾64	9)‾63	8)‾40

Lesson 1 Problem Solving

Solve each problem.

1. There are 18 chairs and 6 tables in the room. There are the same number of chairs at each table. How many chairs are at each table?

   There are _____ chairs.

   There are _____ tables.

   There are _____ chairs at each table.

2. Each box takes 3 min to fill. It took 18 min to fill all the boxes. How many boxes are there?

   It took _____ min to fill all the boxes.

   It takes _____ min to fill one box.

   There are _____ boxes.

3. Rob, Joe, Jay, Tom, Alex, and Jim share six sandwiches. How many sandwiches does each boy get?

   There are _____ sandwiches in all.

   The sandwiches are shared among _____ boys.

   Each boy gets _____ sandwich.

4. Bill and eight friends each sold the same number of tickets. They sold 72 tickets in all. How many tickets were sold by each person?

   Each person sold _____ tickets.

5. Forty-eight oranges are in a crate. The oranges are to be put into bags of six each. How many bags can be filled?

   _____ bags can be filled.

6. Adam has a wire that is 42 cm long. He cuts the wire into 7-cm lengths. How many pieces of wire will he have?

   He will have _____ pieces of wire.

1.

2.

3.

4.

5.

6.

Lesson 2 Division (by 1-digit)

Study how to divide 738 by 3.

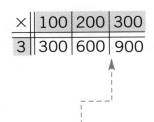

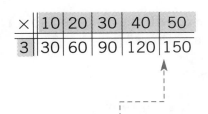

738 is between 600 and 900, so 738 ÷ 3 is between 200 and 300. The hundreds digit is 2.

138 is between 120 and 150, so 138 ÷ 3 is between 40 and 50. The tens digit is 4.

18 ÷ 3 = 6, so the ones digit is 6.

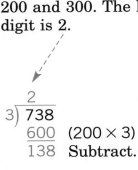

```
  2
3) 738
  600    (200 × 3)
  138    Subtract.
```

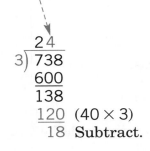

```
   24
3) 738
  600
  138
  120    (40 × 3)
   18    Subtract.
```

```
    246
3) 738
   600
   138
   120
    18
    18    (6 × 3)
```

remainder (r) --→   0   Subtract.

Divide.

	a	b	c	d	e
1.	8)96	4)72	6)72	3)81	4)68
2.	2)74	3)87	5)75	7)784	3)768
3.	8)296	9)315	6)252	6)462	5)930

Lesson 2 Problem Solving

Solve each problem.

1. There are 84 scouts in all. Six will be assigned to each tent. How many tents are there?

   There are _____ scouts in all.

   There are _____ scouts in each tent.

   There are _____ tents.

2. Seven people each worked the same number of hours. They worked 91 h in all. How many hours were worked by each person?

   _____ h were worked.

   _____ people worked these hours.

   _____ h were worked by each person.

3. A group of three is a trio. How many trios could be formed with 72 people?

   _____ trios could be formed.

4. A factory shipped 848 cars to four cities. Each city received the same number of cars. How many cars were shipped to each city?

   _____ cars were shipped.

   _____ cities received the cars.

   _____ cars were shipped to each city.

5. Malcolm, his brother, and his sister have 702 stamps in all. Suppose each takes the same number of stamps. How many will each get?

   Each will get _____ stamps.

6. There are six outs in an inning of baseball. How many innings would have to be played to get 348 outs?

   _____ innings would have to be played.

1.	2.
3.	4.
5.	6.

Lesson 3 Division with Remainders

Study how to divide 854 by 4.

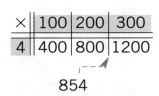

×	100	200	300
4	400	800	1200

854

854÷4 is between 200 and 300. The hundreds digit is 2.

```
    2
4) 854
   800   (200×4)
    54   Subtract.
```

×	10	20	30	40
4	40	80	120	160

54

54÷4 is between 10 and 20. The tens digit is 1.

```
   21
4) 854
   800
    54
    40    (10×4)
    14    Subtract.
```

×	1	2	3	4	5
4	4	8	12	16	20

14

14÷4 is between 3 and 4. The ones digit is 3.

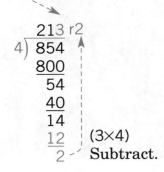

```
   213 r2
4) 854
   800
    54
    40
    14
    12    (3×4)
     2    Subtract.
```

Divide.

	a	b	c	d	e
1.	3) 8 2	5) 8 6	4) 9 7	3) 7 6	2) 4 7
2.	7) 8 3	5) 6 9	6) 2 2 4	4) 1 2 7	2) 3 8 0
3.	4) 2 3 1	5) 6 5 3	7) 9 6 2	2) 4 8 3	6) 8 3 2

Lesson 3 Problem Solving

Solve each problem.

1. There are 160 packages on four large carts. Each
   cart holds the same number of packages. How
   many packages are on each cart?

   Each cart has _____ packages.

1.

2. There are 160 packages. To deliver most of the
   packages, it will take three small planes. Each
   plane will take the same number of packages. How
   many packages will each plane take? How many
   packages will be left over?

   Each plane will take _____ packages.

   There will be _____ package(s) left over.

2.

3. Suppose there had been 890 packages to be
   delivered by six planes. Each plane is to take the
   same number of packages and as many as possible.
   How many packages will each plane take? How
   many will be left over?

   Each plane will take _____ packages.

   There will be _____ packages left over.

3.

Lesson 4   Checking Division

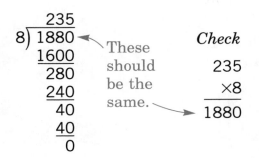

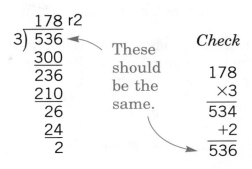

To check $1880 \div 8 = 235$,
   multiply 235 by 8. The answer should be _____.
To check $536 \div 3 = 178$ r2,
   multiply 178 by 3 and then add 2. The answer should be _____.

Divide. Check each answer.

	a	*b*	*c*
1.	$4\overline{)1104}$	$8\overline{)1760}$	$2\overline{)4632}$
2.	$3\overline{)379}$	$5\overline{)421}$	$4\overline{)762}$
3.	$3\overline{)1058}$	$6\overline{)726}$	$7\overline{)2117}$

Lesson 4 Problem Solving

Solve each problem. Check each answer.

1. How many bags of seven oranges each can be filled from a shipment of 341 oranges? How many oranges will be left?

   _____ bags can be filled.

   _____ oranges will be left.

2. Beverly has $2.38 (238¢) to buy pencils for 8¢ each. How many pencils can she buy? How many cents will she have left?

   She can buy _____ pencils.

   She will have _____ ¢ left.

3. There are six stamps in each row. How many complete rows can be filled with 1950 stamps? How many stamps will be left?

   _____ rows will be filled.

   _____ stamps will be left.

4. Daphne had 958 pennies. She exchanged them for nickels. How many nickels did she get? How many pennies did she have left?

   She got _____ nickels.

   She had _____ pennies left.

5. Last year Mr. Gomez worked 1983 h. How many 8-h days was this? How many hours are left?

   It was _____ 8-h days.

   _____ h are left.

6. There are 7633 points to be divided among Paul, Jeremy, and Paige. Each receives the same number of points. How many points will each receive? How many points will be left?

   Each student will receive _____ points.

   _____ point(s) will be left.

1.

2.

3.

4.

5.

6.

Lesson 5   Estimating Quotients

To estimate a quotient, think of a familiar division fact.

$5\overline{)18}$

$\left.\begin{array}{r}4\\5\overline{)20}\\20\\\hline0\end{array}\right\}$ Subtract

Think of what you can round the dividend (18) to so that it is easy to divide mentally by the divisor (5). The quotient is 4.

$7\overline{)342}$

$\left.\begin{array}{r}50\\7\overline{)350}\\350\\\hline0\end{array}\right\}$ Subtract

Think of what you can round the dividend (342) to so that it is easy to divide mentally by the divisor (7). The quotient is 50.

CHAPTER 3

Estimate each quotient.

	a	b	c	d
1.	$4\overline{)25}$	$8\overline{)46}$	$3\overline{)16}$	$9\overline{)48}$
2.	$3\overline{)175}$	$5\overline{)319}$	$7\overline{)236}$	$6\overline{)474}$
3.	$6\overline{)381}$	$4\overline{)316}$	$8\overline{)652}$	$9\overline{)651}$
4.	$2\overline{)1783}$	$6\overline{)2572}$	$5\overline{)4392}$	$4\overline{)4952}$

Lesson 5 Problem Solving

Solve each problem. Use estimation.

1. Brandon bought cookies to pack in his lunch. He bought a box with 28 cookies. If he packs five cookies in his lunch each day, about how many days will the cookies last?

   The cookies will last for about _____ days.

2. Marta babysat for 4 h and earned $19. About how much money did Marta earn each hour that she babysat?

   Marta earned about _____ each hour that she babysat.

3. Bethany rode her bike three days one week. She rode a total of 31 km. If she rode the same distance each day, about how many kilometres did she ride each day that week?

   Bethany rode her bike about _____ km each day that week.

4. Over a 4-week period, Terrell earns $354 at his part-time job. About how much money does Terrell earn each week at his part-time job?

   Terrell earns about _____ each week at his part-time job.

5. The school play was performed five times. For the five performances, there was a total of 962 people in attendance. About how many people were in attendance each time the play was performed?

   There were about _____ people in attendance each time the play was performed.

6. An auditorium holds 1438 people. There are three different sections of seating. Each section has the same number of seats. About how many seats are in each section of the auditorium?

   There are about _____ seats in each section.

1.

2.

3.

4.

5.

6.

CHAPTER 3 PRACTICE TEST
Division (2-digit through 4-digit by 1-digit)

Divide.

	a	*b*	*c*	*d*
1.	$4\overline{)96}$	$7\overline{)84}$	$3\overline{)79}$	$5\overline{)68}$
2.	$4\overline{)732}$	$5\overline{)175}$	$7\overline{)615}$	$2\overline{)647}$
3.	$8\overline{)1720}$	$4\overline{)5216}$	$4\overline{)1530}$	$3\overline{)6323}$
4.	$3\overline{)84}$	$6\overline{)76}$	$8\overline{)94}$	$2\overline{)78}$
5.	$4\overline{)1256}$	$3\overline{)6343}$	$5\overline{)1842}$	$6\overline{)7206}$

CHAPTER 4   PRETEST
Division (2-digit through 4-digit by 2-digit)

Divide.

	a	b	c	d
1.	$13\overline{)78}$	$14\overline{)98}$	$12\overline{)65}$	$15\overline{)95}$
2.	$24\overline{)312}$	$37\overline{)962}$	$12\overline{)586}$	$23\overline{)550}$
3.	$27\overline{)3564}$	$74\overline{)7252}$	$36\overline{)2026}$	$34\overline{)3830}$
4.	$16\overline{)768}$	$52\overline{)2724}$	$18\overline{)310}$	$14\overline{)56}$
5.	$34\overline{)4284}$	$53\overline{)2120}$	$26\overline{)964}$	$11\overline{)418}$

Lesson 1   Division (2-digit)

Study how to divide 94 by 13.
Since $10 \times 13 = 130$ and 130 is greater than 94, there is no tens digit.

13) 9 4

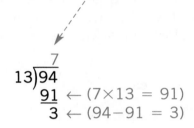

×	1	2	3	4	5	6	7	8
13	13	26	39	52	65	78	91	104

94 is between 91 and 104.
94 ÷ 13 is between 7 and 8.
The *quotient* is 7.

$$\begin{array}{r} 7 \\ 13\overline{)94} \\ \underline{91} \leftarrow (7 \times 13 = 91) \\ 3 \leftarrow (94 - 91 = 3) \end{array}$$

Record the remainder like this.

$$\begin{array}{r} 7 \text{ r3} \\ 13\overline{)94} \\ \underline{91} \\ 3 \end{array}$$ remainder

CHAPTER 4

Divide.

	a	b	c	d	e
1.	12) 8 4	13) 7 8	19) 9 5	16) 8 4	14) 9 8
2.	15) 9 2	14) 7 5	16) 7 4	13) 8 0	12) 9 2
3.	17) 6 8	23) 9 2	32) 8 4	18) 7 2	27) 9 1

Lesson 1 Problem Solving

Solve each problem.

1. The pet store has 84 birds. They have 14 large cages. There are the same number of birds in each cage. How many birds are in each cage?

   _____ birds are in each cage.

2. The pet store also has 63 kittens. There are 12 cages with the same number of kittens in each. The rest of the kittens are in the display window. How many kittens are in each cage? How many kittens are in the display window?

   _____ kittens are in each cage.

   _____ kittens are in the display window.

3. There are 60 guppies in a large tank. If the pet store puts 15 guppies each in a smaller tank, how many smaller tanks will be needed?

   _____ smaller tanks will be needed.

4. There are 72 boxes of pet food on a shelf. The boxes are in rows of 13 each. How many full rows of boxes are there? How many boxes are left over?

   There are _____ full rows of boxes.

   There are _____ boxes left over.

5. There are 80 cages to be cleaned. Each of the store's 19 employees is to clean the same number of cages. The owner will clean any leftover cages. How many cages will each employee clean? How many cages will the owner clean?

   Each employee will clean _____ cages.

   The owner will clean _____ cages.

6. There are 52 puppies. There are 13 cages. If each cage contains the same number of puppies, how many puppies are in each cage?

   There are _____ puppies in each cage.

| 1. |
| 2. |
| 3. |
| 4. |
| 5. |
| 6. |

Lesson 2 Division (3-digit)

Study how to divide 219 by 12 .

×	10	20	30	40
12	120	240	360	480

↑ 219

219 ÷ 12 is between 10 and 20.
The tens digit is 1.

```
      1
12) 2 1 9
    1 2 0
      9 9
```

×	1	2	3	4	5	6	7	8	9
12	12	24	36	48	60	72	84	96	108

99 - - - - - - - - - →

99 ÷ 12 is between 8 and 9.
The ones digit is 8.

```
      18 r3
12) 2 1 9
    1 2 0
      9 9
      9 6
        3
```

Divide.

	a	*b*	*c*	*d*	*e*
1.	13) 3 5 1	16) 2 5 6	17) 3 2 3	14) 4 9 0	12) 8 1 4

2.	26) 3 1 6	31) 4 1 3	17) 2 1 2	24) 3 6 0	28) 5 6 4

Lesson 2 Problem Solving

Solve each problem.

1. There are 448 packages of paper in the supply room. Fourteen packages are used each day. At that rate, how many days will the supply of paper last?

The supply of paper will last _____ days.

2. There are 338 cases on a truck. The truck will make 12 stops and leave the same number of cases at each stop. How many cases will be left at each stop? How many cases will still be on the truck?

_____ cases will be left at each stop.

_____ cases will still be on the truck.

3. There are 582 tickets to be sold. Each of 24 students is to receive the same number of tickets and sell as many as possible. The teacher is to sell any tickets left over. How many tickets is each student to sell? How many is the teacher to sell?

Each student is to sell _____ tickets.

The teacher is to sell _____ tickets.

4. A machine operated 38 h and produced 988 parts. The same number of parts was produced each hour. How many parts were produced each hour?

_____ parts were produced each hour.

5. After 24 h, the machine in problem **4** had produced 582 parts. About how many parts is the machine producing each hour? Is it producing at the rate it is designed to do?

About _____ parts are being produced each hour.

6. Suppose the machine in problem **4** was operated 19 h. During this time 988 parts were produced. The same number of parts was produced each hour. How many were produced each hour?

_____ parts were produced each hour.

1.
2.
3.
4.
5.
6.

Lesson 3 Division (3-digit)

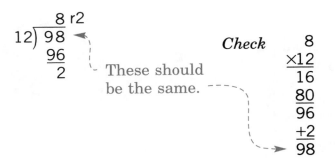

```
      8 r2
12) 98
    96
     2
```
These should be the same.

Check
```
      8
    ×12
     16
     80
     96
     +2
     98
```

To check 98 ÷ 12 = 8 r2, multiply 8

by _____ and add _____ to that product.

The answer should be _____.

```
      12
34) 408
    340
     68
     68
      0
```
These should be the same.

Check
```
     12
    ×34
     48
    360
    408
```

To check 408 ÷ 34 = 12, multiply 12

by _____. The answer should be _____.

Divide. Check each answer.

	a	*b*	*c*
1.	16) 8 8	14) 8 4	23) 9 4
2.	19) 1 1 4	36) 7 5 6	32) 8 3 6
3.	25) 3 3 0	36) 6 7 2	45) 8 1 0

Lesson 3 Problem Solving

Solve each problem. Check each answer.

1. Lucinda had 59¢ to buy pencils that cost 14¢ each. How many pencils could she buy? How many cents would she have left?

   She could buy _____ pencils.

   She would have _____¢ left.

2. The grocer has 98 cans of beans to put on a shelf. He thinks he can put 16 cans in each row. If he does, how many rows will he have? How many cans will be left?

   He will have _____ rows.

   _____ cans will be left.

3. The grocer in problem 2 could only put 13 cans in each row. How many rows does he have? How many cans are left?

   He has _____ rows.

   _____ cans are left.

4. There are 774 cartons ready for shipment. Only 27 cartons can be shipped on each truck. How many full truckloads will there be? How many cartons will be left?

   There will be _____ full loads.

   _____ cartons will be left.

5. There are 605 books in the storage room. There are the same number of books in each of 17 full boxes and the rest in an extra box. How many books are in each full box? How many books are in the extra box?

   _____ books are in each full box.

   _____ books are in the extra box.

| 1. |
| 2. |
| 3. |
| 4. |
| 5. |

Lesson 4 Division (4-digit)

Study how to divide 8550 by 25.

×	100	200	300	400
25	2500	5000	7500	10 000

8550 ⤴

The hundreds digit is 3.

```
    3
25) 8550
    7500
    1050
```

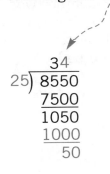

×	10	20	30	40	50
25	250	500	750	1000	1250

1050 ⤴

The tens digit is 4.

```
    34
25) 8550
    7500
    1050
    1000
      50
```

×	1	2
25	25	50

50 ⤴

The ones digit is 2.

```
    342
25) 8550
    7500
    1050
    1000
      50
      50
       0
```

Divide.

	a	*b*	*c*	*d*
1.	32) 5 2 8 0	43) 6 7 5 1	26) 6 3 1 8	75) 9 1 5 0
2.	42) 8 9 5 6	31) 9 8 7 5	23) 3 8 4 4	63) 9 0 0 8
3.	35) 1 9 6 0	75) 3 9 0 0	63) 2 6 5 6	27) 1 4 3 0

Lesson 4 Problem Solving

Solve each problem.

1. A truck is loaded with 8073 kg of food. Each case of
   food has a mass of 23 kg. How many cases are on
   the truck?

   _____ cases are on the truck.

2. During an 8-h shift, one machine was able to
   package 8215 boxes of rice. These boxes were packed
   24 to a carton. How many full cartons of rice would
   this be? How many boxes would be left?

   There would be _____ full cartons.

   _____ boxes would be left.

3. The bakery uses 75 kg of butter in each batch of
   butter-bread dough. How many batches of dough
   could be made with 6300 kg of butter?

   _____ batches of dough could be made.

4. There are 2030 students in a school. How many
   classes of 28 students each could there be? How
   many students would be left?

   There could be _____ full classes.

   _____ students would be left.

5. In 27 days 3888 L of oil were used. The same
   amount of oil was used each day. How much oil was
   used each day?

   _____ L were used each day.

6. There are 5100 parts to be packed. The parts are to
   be packed 24 to a box. How many boxes can be
   filled? How many parts will be left?

   _____ full boxes will be packed.

   _____ parts will be left.

1.
2.
3.
4.
5.
6.

Lesson 5 Division (2-, 3-, and 4-digit)

Divide.

	a	b	c	d
1.	$28\overline{)776}$	$42\overline{)5176}$	$19\overline{)95}$	$33\overline{)133}$
2.	$12\overline{)2606}$	$22\overline{)6754}$	$24\overline{)792}$	$11\overline{)1716}$
3.	$14\overline{)84}$	$89\overline{)801}$	$75\overline{)753}$	$16\overline{)2616}$
4.	$75\overline{)6375}$	$23\overline{)5543}$	$25\overline{)8000}$	$25\overline{)800}$
5.	$15\overline{)6009}$	$60\overline{)1860}$	$20\overline{)7020}$	$48\overline{)1704}$

CHAPTER 4

Lesson 5 Problem Solving

<table>
<tr><td>ORDER FORM</td></tr>
<tr><td>6912 Zanappas</td></tr>
</table>

Solve each problem.

1. An order was received for 6912 zanappas. Machine A can produce the zanappas in 12 h. At that rate, how many zanappas would be produced each hour?

   _____ zanappas would be produced each hour.

2. It would take Machine B 24 h to produce the zanappas needed to fill the order. At that rate, how many zanappas would be produced each hour?

   _____ zanappas would be produced each hour.

3. Machine C could produce the zanappas needed to fill the order in 48 h. At that rate, how many zanappas could be produced each hour?

   _____ zanappas could be produced each hour.

4. How many zanappas could be produced if all three machines operated for a period of 8 h?

   _____ zanappas could be produced.

1.	2.
3.	4.

CHAPTER 4   PRACTICE TEST
Division (2-digit through 4-digit by 2-digit)

Divide.

	a	*b*	*c*	*d*
1.	12)‾7‾2‾	13)‾8‾9‾	11)‾9‾4‾	17)‾6‾8‾
2.	17)‾2‾6‾5‾	11)‾8‾5‾8‾	31)‾9‾6‾1‾	12)‾5‾0‾6‾
3.	36)‾4‾3‾6‾6‾	42)‾1‾8‾9‾0‾	73)‾3‾9‾3‾4‾	14)‾2‾1‾8‾4‾
4.	13)‾1‾6‾9‾	26)‾3‾1‾7‾5‾	16)‾7‾5‾	36)‾1‾4‾4‾
5.	54)‾1‾4‾5‾8‾	25)‾2‾0‾9‾5‾	28)‾5‾7‾3‾	42)‾9‾9‾

CHAPTER 5   PRETEST
Division (4- and 5-digit by 2-digit)

Divide.

	a	*b*	*c*	*d*
1.	25$)\overline{75}$	25$)\overline{750}$	25$)\overline{7500}$	25$)\overline{75\,000}$
2.	38$)\overline{4256}$	17$)\overline{4033}$	33$)\overline{7326}$	25$)\overline{2145}$
3.	42$)\overline{89\,523}$	16$)\overline{97\,978}$	25$)\overline{62\,940}$	15$)\overline{31\,762}$
4.	27$)\overline{12\,204}$	48$)\overline{27\,648}$	62$)\overline{19\,664}$	72$)\overline{31\,968}$

Lesson 1 Division (5-digit)

Study how to divide 24 567 by 12.

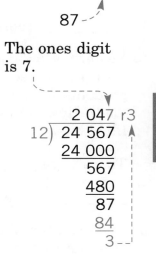

×	1000	2000	3000
12	12 000	24 000	36 000

24 567

The thousands digit is 2.

```
         2
12) 24 567
    24 000
       567
```

×	100	200
12	1200	2400

567 ÷ 12 is less than 100. The hundreds digit is 0.

```
        2 0
12) 24 567
    24 000
       567
```

×	30	40	50
12	360	480	600

567

The tens digit is 4.

```
        2 04
12) 24 567
    24 000
       567
       480
        87
```

×	6	7	8
12	72	84	96

87

The ones digit is 7.

```
        2 047 r3
12) 24 567
    24 000
       567
       480
        87
        84
         3
```

Divide.

	a	*b*	*c*	*d*
1.	36) 4 5 0 0	26) 8 4 3 0	92) 7 9 1 1	25) 3 5 7 5
2.	24) 7 7 1 8 4	92) 3 9 7 5 4	56) 6 9 1 0 4	23) 1 7 3 4 2

Lesson 1 Problem Solving

Solve each problem.

1. In 27 days, 6939 orders were filled. The same number of orders was filled each day. How many orders were filled each day?

   _____ orders were filled each day.

   1.

2. Yesterday 5650 school children came in buses to visit the museum. How many full bus loads of students were there if 75 students make up a full load? How many students were on the partially filled bus?

   There were _____ full bus loads.

   _____ students were on the partially filled bus.

   2.

3. The inventory slip shows that there are 7840 pairs of socks in the warehouse. There are 32 pairs in each box. How many boxes of socks should there be in the warehouse?

   There should be _____ boxes of socks.

   3.

4. A factory produced 7605 zimbits yesterday. The zimbits are packed 24 to a box. How many full boxes of zimbits were produced? How many zimbits were left?

   There were _____ full boxes.

   _____ zimbits were left.

   4.

5. The stadium is separated into 16 sections. Each section has the same number of seats. There are 8640 seats in all. How many seats are in each section?

   There are _____ seats in each section.

   5.

6. Suppose there were 9600 seats in the stadium in problem **5**. How many seats would be in each section?

   There would be _____ seats in each section.

   6.

Lesson 2 Division (5-digit)

Study how to divide 24 205 by 75.

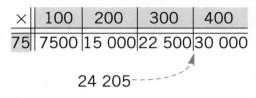

×	100	200	300	400
75	7500	15 000	22 500	30 000

24 205 - - - - →

The hundreds digit is 3.

```
         3
75) 24 205
    22 500
     1 705
```

×	10	20	30	40
75	750	1500	2250	3000

1705

The tens digit is 2.

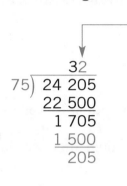

```
        32
75) 24 205
    22 500
     1 705
     1 500
       205
```

×	1	2	3	4
75	75	150	225	300

205

The ones digit is 2.

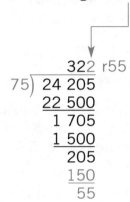

```
       322 r55
75) 24 205
    22 500
     1 705
     1 500
       205
       150
        55
```

Divide.

	a	*b*	*c*	*d*
1.	43) 17 716	64) 32 768	27) 22 005	28) 60 088
2.	33) 27 313	31) 96 843	43) 89 800	59) 41 645

Lesson 2 Problem Solving

Solve each problem.

1. A bus can carry 86 passengers. How many such buses would be needed to carry 20 898 passengers?

   _____ buses would be needed.

   1.

2. There are 16 oranges in one bag. How many bags are there if there are 39 238 oranges? How many oranges are left?

   There are _____ bags.

   There are _____ oranges left.

   2.

3. There are 31 500 kg of salt to be put into bags with 36 kg in each bag. How many full bags of salt would there be? How many kilograms would be left?

   There would be _____ full bags.

   _____ kg would be left.

   3.

4. It takes 72 h for one machine to produce 14 616 parts. The machine produces the same number of parts each hour. How many parts does it produce each hour?

   It produces _____ parts each hour.

   4.

5. Suppose the machine in problem 4 could produce the parts in 36 h. How many parts would it produce each hour?

   It would produce _____ parts each hour.

   5.

6. Suppose the machine in problem 4 could produce the parts in 18 h. How many parts would it produce each hour?

   It would produce _____ parts each hour.

   6.

7. Suppose the machine in problem 4 could produce the parts in 12 h. How many parts would it produce each hour?

   It would produce _____ parts each hour.

   7.

Lesson 3   Checking Division

```
        2 543 r8                    Check
  16) 40 696 ◄                              To check 40 696 ÷ 16 = 2543 r8, multiply
      32 000                          2 543
       8 696      These               ×16        2543 by _____ and then add _____ to this
       8 000      should           15 258
         696      be the           25 430        product. The answer should be _____ .
         640      same.            40 688
          56                          +8
          48                       40 696
           8
```

Divide. Check each answer.

	a	*b*
1.	47) 99 932	54) 33 100
2.	38) 27 590	46) 38 277
3.	75) 95 100	24) 30 900

Lesson 3 Problem Solving

Solve each problem. Check each answer.

1. There are 35 gates into the stadium and 15 330 people attended the game. The same number entered through each gate. How many entered through each gate?

_____ people entered through each gate.

2. A garage used 16 434 L of oil in 83 days. The same amount of oil was used each day. How much oil was used each day?

_____ L were used each day.

3. During 6 months, 77 employees worked 67 639 h. Suppose each employee worked the same number of hours. How many hours did each work? How many hours would be left?

Each employee worked _____ h.

_____ h are left.

4. Ninety-five containers of the same size were filled with a total of 82 840 kg of coal. How many kilograms of coal were in each container?

_____ kg were in each container.

5. There are 46 963 students attending 52 schools in the city. Suppose the same number attend each school. How many students would attend each school? How many would be left?

_____ students would attend each school.

_____ students would be left.

6. Suppose there were twice as many students in problem 5. How many students would attend each school? How many would be left?

_____ students would attend each school.

_____ students would be left.

1.
2.
3.
4.
5.
6.

Lesson 4   Division (4- and 5-digit)

Divide.

	a	b	c	d
1.	38$\overline{)72}$	23$\overline{)601}$	32$\overline{)4640}$	34$\overline{)43\,877}$
2.	24$\overline{)54}$	24$\overline{)540}$	24$\overline{)5400}$	24$\overline{)54\,000}$
3.	12$\overline{)87}$	21$\overline{)168}$	42$\overline{)1491}$	38$\overline{)21\,584}$
4.	87$\overline{)95}$	24$\overline{)369}$	75$\overline{)6005}$	45$\overline{)30\,605}$

Lesson 4 Problem Solving

Solve each problem.

1. Hannah is to read 228 pages in four sessions. She will read the same number of pages each session. How many pages will she read each session?

   She will read _____ pages each session.

   1.

2. The square of a number is found by multiplying the number by itself. Matthew said that 2916 is the square of 54. Is he right?

   Matthew _____ right.

   2.

3. The astronauts are now 8640 min into their flight. How many hours is this? How many days?

   It is _____ h.

   It is _____ days.

   3.

4. In 5 hours 15 190 cans came off the assembly line. There are 88 cans packed in each carton. How many full cartons are there? How many cans are in the partially filled carton?

   There are _____ full cartons.

   There are _____ cans in the partial carton.

   4.

5. A satellite has just completed its 94th orbit. It has been in orbit for 8460 min. How long does it take to make a complete orbit?

   It takes _____ min to make one orbit.

   5.

6. How long will the satellite in problem **5** have been in orbit after it has completed its 100th orbit?

   It will have been in orbit _____ h.

   6.

CHAPTER 5   PRACTICE TEST
Division (4- and 5-digit by 2-digit)

Divide.

	a	*b*	*c*	*d*
1.	$97\overline{)873}$	$56\overline{)952}$	$70\overline{)2870}$	$63\overline{)6615}$
2.	$31\overline{)8308}$	$41\overline{)5043}$	$11\overline{)1232}$	$77\overline{)9831}$
3.	$32\overline{)23744}$	$93\overline{)31657}$	$51\overline{)21483}$	$43\overline{)31605}$
4.	$25\overline{)23375}$	$17\overline{)34096}$	$37\overline{)65510}$	$77\overline{)92324}$
5.	$35\overline{)35035}$	$25\overline{)10025}$	$31\overline{)93006}$	$13\overline{)10413}$

CHAPTER 6 PRETEST
Money

In each dollar amount, circle the digit in the given place value.

	a	*b*
1.	$345.06; hundredths place	$705.98; tenths place
2.	$4587.91; tens place	$135.74; hundreds place

Express each dollar amount in standard form.

3. eighty-three dollars and seventy-five cents $83.75

4. seven hundred sixty-three dollars and forty-nine cents $763.49

Add.

	a	*b*	*c*	*d*	*e*
5.	$2.94 +6.18 $9.12	$32.05 +18.76 $50.81	$267.31 +46.98 $314.29	$319.46 +229.35 $548.81	$4864.11 +2417.39 $7281.50

Subtract.

6.	$9.41 −3.18 $6.23	$33.29 −28.47 $4.82	$705.92 −56.35 $649.57	$468.13 −125.26 $342.83	$5671.48 −3489.17

Multiply.

7.	$1.38 ×4 $5.52	$8.63 ×7 $60.41	$37.81 ×5 $185.05	$5.49 ×21	$55.19 ×38

Divide.

8. 3)$0.87   8)$9.84   6)$34.56   14)$7.56   47)$99.64

Lesson 1 Place Value

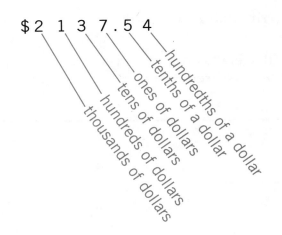

In $6043.25, what number is in the tenths place?

__2__ is in the tenths place.

In each dollar amount, circle the digit in the given place value.

a

1. $194.28; ones place
2. $3581.06; hundredths place
3. $264.97; hundreds place
4. $6804.15; tenths place
5. $3248.05; thousands place
6. $5810.64; hundredths place
7. $315.42; ones place
8. $7241.36; tens place
9. $5316.24; hundreds place
10. $516.37; tenths place
11. $4256.38; hundredths place
12. $1834.90; thousands place

b

$3829.76; hundreds place

$815.49; tens place

$5216.38; tenths place

$197.32; ones place

$8213.45; hundredths place

$2183.67; thousands place

$467.03; tenths place

$3425.10; ones place

$365.42; hundreds place

$9216.35; hundredths place

$8093.17; tens place

$6314.25; thousands place

Lesson 2 Writing Money

Write "two hundred eighteen dollars and thirty-seven cents" in standard form.

$218.37

Write $58.23 in word form.

Fifty-eight dollars and twenty-three cents.

Express each dollar amount in standard form.

1. thirty-seven dollars and twenty-six cents _____

2. seventy-two dollars and sixty-one cents _____

3. four hundred twenty-one dollars and thirty-five cents _____

4. five hundred forty-four dollars and thirteen cents _____

5. nine hundred eighty-one dollars and ninety cents _____

6. two thousand, seven hundred thirty-six dollars and forty-five cents _____

Express each dollar amount in word form.

7. $41.57 _____

8. $30.24 _____

9. $652.74 _____

10. $426.13 _____

11. $703.89 _____

12. $3950.21 _____

Lesson 3   Addition of Money

To add money, line up the decimal points. Then add from right to left.

$1.29	$1.²9	$1.¹ ¹29	$1.29
+0.84	+0.84	+0,84	+0.84
	3	.13	$2.13

Add.

	a	b	c	d	e
1.	$0.42	$6.90	$3.45	$6.08	$3.12
	+1.83	+2.63	+7.32	+0.73	+9.76
2.	$21.54	$42.81	$15.64	$46.81	$62.18
	+18.13	+37.52	+12.21	+19.84	+73.48
3.	$623.65	$483.21	$265.95	$80.21	$28.35
	+82.79	+21.19	+38.41	+363.14	+917.64
4.	$648.15	$345.61	$483.85	$724.31	$511.29
	+794.05	+725.88	+297.65	+613.55	+180.46
5.	$2316.25	$4866.23	$4786.03	$5024.87	$1358.01
	+6108.34	+1585.50	+4671.29	+1094.71	+8274.81
6.	$52.64	$13.29	$243.25	$2268.06	$4545.19
	77.64	264.08	71.78	411.52	6133.41
	+29.05	+38.27	+883.40	+4186.54	+8009.77

CHAPTER 6

Lesson 3 Problem Solving

Solve each problem.

1. At the convenience store, Danielle bought 2 L of milk that cost $2.85 and a bag of pretzels that cost $1.99. How much money did Danielle spend at the convenience store?

Danielle spent _____ at the convenience store.

1.

2. On Friday night, Wynona earned $11.75 baby-sitting. On Saturday afternoon, she earned $5.50 helping her neighbor clean her house. How much money did Wynona earn on Friday and Saturday?

Wynona earned _____ on Friday and Saturday.

2.

3. Justin bought a bike that cost $128.50 and a helmet that cost $29.75. How much money did Justin spend on the bike and helmet?

Justin spent _____ on the bike and helmet.

3.

4. Jamar went to the deli for lunch. He bought a sandwich for $2.75, a bag of chips for $0.80, and a fruit juice for $1.35. How much money did Jamar spend at the deli for lunch?

Jamar spent _____ at the deli for lunch.

4.

5. Kyle has money in a chequing account and a savings account. He has $348.12 in his chequing account and $1069.57 in his savings account. How much money does Kyle have in his two accounts?

Kyle has _____ in his two accounts.

5.

6. Ramona is a salesperson. In January, her sales total was $6458.24. In February, her sales total was $8058.75. What was Ramona's sales total for January and February?

Ramona's sales total for January and February was _____.

6.

Lesson 4   Subtraction of Money

To subtract money, line up the decimal points. Then subtract from right to left.

$$\begin{array}{r} \$15.65 \\ -7.49 \\ \hline \end{array} \qquad \begin{array}{r} {}^{515} \\ \$15.\cancel{65} \\ -7.49 \\ \hline 6 \end{array} \qquad \begin{array}{r} {}^{515} \\ \$15.\cancel{65} \\ -7.49 \\ \hline .16 \end{array} \qquad \begin{array}{r} {}^{015\ 515} \\ \$1\cancel{5}.\cancel{65} \\ -7.49 \\ \hline \$8.16 \end{array}$$

Subtract.

	a	b	c	d	e
1.	$6.84 −1.19	$9.59 −5.75	$5.02 −3.18	$4.53 −3.26	$7.27 −6.98
2.	$45.34 −17.50	$12.80 −7.41	$78.46 −34.85	$41.63 −39.45	$56.42 −34.13
3.	$345.91 −97.37	$469.25 −57.36	$427.63 −90.47	$727.44 −78.34	$410.65 −99.27
4.	$764.33 −551.92	$604.15 −538.22	$926.40 −674.12	$541.73 −336.95	$831.92 −624.51
5.	$3068.15 −715.94	$5943.05 −843.16	$3128.65 −461.08	$4216.38 −530.08	$8003.69 −742.31
6.	$3450.18 −2290.46	$5024.88 −2656.28	$8124.77 −7653.25	$1192.06 −1086.33	$9624.08 −3782.14

CHAPTER 6

Lesson 4 Problem Solving

Solve each problem.

1. On Wednesday, Caroline spent $3.80 for lunch. On Thursday, she spent $5.25 for lunch. How much more money did Caroline spend on Thursday for lunch than on Wednesday?

   Caroline spent _____ more on Thursday for lunch than on Wednesday.

   1.

2. At Pete's Pizzeria, a large pizza costs $12.50. A medium pizza costs $8.75. How much more does a large pizza cost than a medium pizza at Pete's Pizzeria?

   A large pizza costs _____ more than a medium pizza at Pete's Pizzeria.

   2.

3. Singh and Patrick went to a music store. Singh bought a CD that cost $17.50. Patrick bought a CD that cost $12.99. How much more did Singh spend than Patrick?

   Singh spent _____ more for his CD than Patrick.

   3.

4. Keung earns $13.50 for mowing his grandmother's lawn. He earns $15.00 for mowing his neighbour's lawn. How much more money does Keung earn for mowing his neighbour's lawn than he does for mowing his grandmother's lawn?

   Keung earns _____ more for mowing his neighbour's lawn.

   4.

5. Rachel has $564.12 in her savings account. Mitchell has $392.46 in his savings account. How much more money does Rachel have in her savings account than Mitchell?

   Rachel has _____ more in her savings account.

   5.

6. Jasmine bought a car for $9867.50. She sold her old car for $3575.00. She used all the money from selling her old car as a deposit for her new car. After the deposit, how much more money did Jasmine have to pay for her new car?

   Jasmine had to pay _____ more for her new car.

   6.

Lesson 5 Multiplication of Money

Multiply money the same way you multiply with whole numbers.

$$\begin{array}{r}{\scriptstyle 3}\\ \$2.85\\ \times 6\\ \hline 0\end{array} \quad \begin{array}{r}{\scriptstyle 5\ 3}\\ \$2.85\\ \times 6\\ \hline 10\end{array} \quad \begin{array}{r}{\scriptstyle 5\ 3}\\ \$2.85 \leftarrow 2\text{ decimal places}\\ \times 6\\ \hline \$17.10 \leftarrow 2\text{ decimal places}\end{array}$$

Be sure to include the dollar sign and decimal point in your answer.

Multiply 835 by 4. Then multiply 835 by 20. Add. Then write the dollar sign and decimal point.

2 decimal places ⟶ $8.35
×24
3340 ⎫ Add.
16700 ⎭
2 decimal places → $200.40

Multiply.

	a	b	c	d	e
1.	$1.15 ×3	$3.68 ×8	$6.52 ×7	$1.33 ×9	$9.11 ×5
2.	$25.48 ×7	$74.12 ×2	$65.43 ×5	$45.35 ×4	$39.04 ×9
3.	$6.27 ×18	$9.25 ×34	$8.45 ×52	$31.60 ×94	$79.25 ×21
4.	$65.80 ×35	$33.64 ×68	$27.81 ×41	$13.62 ×185	$84.67 ×315

Lesson 5 Problem Solving

Solve each problem.

1. Apples are on sale for $0.99 per kilogram. Zach bought 3 kg of apples. How much money did Zach spend on the apples?

   Zach spent _____ on the apples.

2. At the concession stand, hot dogs cost $1.25. Mr. Garcia bought six hot dogs for his family. How much did Mr. Garcia pay for the hot dogs?

   Mr. Garcia paid _____ for the hot dogs.

3. Natasha earns $4.25 an hour for babysitting. If Natasha babysits for 5 h, how much money does she earn?

   Natasha earns _____ for babysitting 5 h.

4. Michael bought 15 packs of baseball cards. If each pack costs $1.95, how much money did Michael spend on the baseball cards?

   Michael spent _____ on the baseball cards.

5. Jenny earns $325.72 each month at her part-time job. How much money does Jenny earn in one year at her job?

   Jenny earns _____ in one year.

6. At a rental car company, it costs $26.80 per day to rent a mid-size car. Lamar rented a mid-size car from this company for 14 days. How much did Lamar spend for the rental car?

   Lamar spent _____ for the rental car.

7. A company had a summer picnic for its employees. The food for the picnic was catered. The food cost $3.75 per person. If there were 264 people at the picnic, what was the total cost for the food?

   The total cost for the food at the company picnic was _____.

1.

2.

3.

4.

5.

6.

7.

Lesson 6 Division of Money

When dividing money, place the decimal point in the quotient over the decimal point in the dividend. Then divide as if you were dividing whole numbers.

$$
\begin{array}{r} 6)\overline{\$2.58} \end{array}
\qquad
\begin{array}{r} \$0.4 \\ 6)\overline{\$2.58} \\ 240 \end{array}
\qquad
\begin{array}{r} \$0.4 \\ 6)\overline{\$2.58} \\ 240 \\ \hline 18 \end{array} \Big\} \text{Subtract.}
\qquad
\begin{array}{r} \$0.43 \\ 6)\overline{\$2.58} \\ 240 \\ \hline 18 \\ 18 \\ \hline 0 \end{array} \Big\} \text{Subtract.}
$$

Divide.

	a	b	c	d	e
1.	$4)\overline{\$0.68}$	$8)\overline{\$1.04}$	$6)\overline{\$1.32}$	$5)\overline{\$0.90}$	$7)\overline{\$3.01}$
2.	$8)\overline{\$4.24}$	$3)\overline{\$2.88}$	$7)\overline{\$6.09}$	$4)\overline{\$5.32}$	$9)\overline{\$7.38}$
3.	$7)\overline{\$20.86}$	$5)\overline{\$33.85}$	$4)\overline{\$73.72}$	$3)\overline{\$74.97}$	$6)\overline{\$75.48}$
4.	$23)\overline{\$8.28}$	$16)\overline{\$7.20}$	$34)\overline{\$8.84}$	$12)\overline{\$5.28}$	$28)\overline{\$9.52}$
5.	$42)\overline{\$90.72}$	$85)\overline{\$55.25}$	$33)\overline{\$98.01}$	$62)\overline{\$96.10}$	$31)\overline{\$85.87}$

CHAPTER 6

Lesson 6 Problem Solving

Solve each problem.

1. Kathy bought four cucumbers at the produce store for $2.36. How much did each cucumber cost?

   Each cucumber cost _____ at the produce store.

2. Nestor earned $14.00 for helping his elderly neighbour do yardwork for 4 h. How much did Nestor earn each hour?

   Nestor earned _____ each hour he helped his neighbour.

3. Maria spent $14.75 on five packs of thank-you cards. How much did each pack of thank-you cards cost?

   Each pack of thank-you cards cost _____.

4. For a school fundraiser, Jeremy sold 34 chocolate bars. He collected $42.50 for the chocolate bars he sold. How much did each chocolate bar cost?

   Each chocolate bar cost _____.

5. Tina bought six pairs of socks for $14.94. How much did each pair of socks cost?

   Each pair of socks cost _____.

6. Naoko bought three new pairs of khaki pants for work. He spent $71.85 for all three pairs. How much did each pair of pants cost?

   Each pair of pants cost _____.

7. The community service club had a fundraiser to raise money for three local charities. They raised $98.61. If they split the money equally among the three charities, how much money will each charity receive?

   Each charity will receive _____ from the community service club.

1.

2.

3.

4.

5.

6.

7.

Lesson 7 Problem Solving

Mariana bought a pair of shoes for $26.85. Two weeks later, Mariana's friend Lauren bought the same pair of shoes for $21.58. How much more did Mariana pay for the pair of shoes than Lauren?

Are you to add or subtract? _subtract_

Mariana paid __$5.27__ more for the shoes than Lauren.

Subtract the two amounts to find out how much more Mariana paid for the shoes than Lauren.

$$\begin{array}{r} {\scriptstyle 715} \\ \$26.\cancel{8}\cancel{5} \\ -21.58 \\ \hline 7 \end{array} \qquad \begin{array}{r} {\scriptstyle 715} \\ \$26.\cancel{8}\cancel{5} \\ -21.58 \\ \hline .27 \end{array} \qquad \begin{array}{r} {\scriptstyle 715} \\ \$26.\cancel{8}\cancel{5} \\ -21.58 \\ \hline \$5.27 \end{array}$$

Answer each question.

1. The soccer coach bought five soccer balls for his team. If each soccer ball costs $12.95, how much will the coach spend for five soccer balls?

   Are you to multiply or divide? _____

   How much will the coach spend for five soccer balls? _____

   1.

2. Madeline bought a picture frame that cost $7.65. She paid with a $10 bill. How much change did Madeline get back?

   Are you to add or subtract? _____

   How much change did Madeline get back?

   _____

   2.

3. Charlie bought six tickets to the school play for $22.50. How much did each ticket cost?

   Are you to multiply or divide? _____

   How much did each ticket cost? _____

   3.

4. Vanessa went to the pet store and bought a new collar for her dog that cost $5.95. She also bought a bag of food that cost $12.16. How much money did Vanessa spend at the pet store?

   Are you to add or subtract? _____

   How much money did Vanessa spend at the pet store? _____

   4.

Lesson 7 Problem Solving

Answer each question.

1. Maya earns $6.22 per hour at her part-time job. Nicole earns $5.17 per hour at her part-time job. How much more per hour does Maya earn at her part-time job than Nicole?

Are you to add or subtract? _____

How much more per hour does Maya earn at her part-time job than Nicole? _____

2. Brian spent $14.37 for 3 kg of ham at the deli. How much does 1 kg of ham cost at the deli?

Are you to multiply or divide? _____

How much does 1 kg of ham cost at the deli? _____

3. Clara went shopping at the mall. She bought a sweater that cost $24.99, a pair of sunglasses that cost $12.65, and a pair of earrings that cost $6.20. How much money did Clara spend at the mall?

Are you to add or subtract? _____

How much did Clara spend at the mall? _____

4. At the school cafeteria, a slice of pizza costs $1.35 and a hamburger costs $2.60. How much more does a hamburger cost than a slice of pizza at the school cafeteria?

Are you to add or subtract? _____

How much more does a hamburger cost than a slice of pizza at the school cafeteria? _____

5. Rashad bought an 8-kg turkey at the grocery store. It was on sale for $1.79 per kilogram. How much did Rashad spend on the turkey?

Are you to multiply or divide? _____

How much did Rashad spend on the turkey?

_____

1.

2.

3.

4.

5.

CHAPTER 6   PRACTICE TEST
Money

In each dollar amount, circle the digit in the given place value.

a	b

1. $903.48; ones place $673.19; hundredths place

2. $8364.82; tenths place $1813.06; thousands place

Express each dollar amount in standard form.

3. thirty-four dollars and seventy-two cents _____

4. two hundred fifteen dollars and ninety-one cents _____

Add.

	a	b	c	d	e
5.	$2.59 +8.43	$27.64 +71.09	$684.05 +83.47	$187.46 +456.45	$1845.54 +9453.72

Subtract.

	a	b	c	d	e
6.	$7.94 −4.57	$79.18 −53.22	$619.06 −74.25	$914.47 −294.51	$7064.38 −2271.45

Multiply.

	a	b	c	d	e
7.	$1.07 ×6	$6.19 ×4	$29.67 ×8	$7.85 ×36	$24.92 ×28

Divide.

8. $6\overline{)\$0.96}$ $7\overline{)\$9.94}$ $5\overline{)\$56.85}$ $26\overline{)\$9.10}$ $21\overline{)\$90.93}$

CHAPTER 6

CHAPTER 7   PRETEST
Graphs and Averages

Use the bar graph to answer each question.

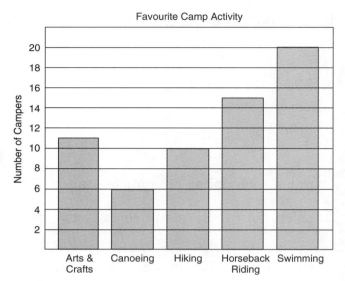

1. How many campers chose canoeing as their favourite activity? _____

2. How many campers chose horseback riding as their favourite activity? _____

3. How many more campers chose arts and crafts as their favourite activity than hiking? _____

4. How many fewer campers chose canoeing as their favourite activity than swimming? _____

Use the line graph to answer each question.

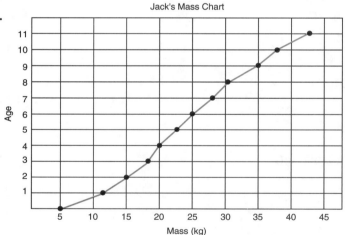

5. What was Jack's mass when he was 2 years old? _____

6. What was Jack's mass when he was 10 years old? _____

7. How much more was Jack's mass when he was 9 years old than when he was 5 years old? _____

Find the mean, median, mode, and range of each set of numbers.

	a		*b*

8. 3, 7, 3, 8, 9   mean: _____   13, 19, 15, 22, 14, 19, 17   mean: _____

   median: _____   median: _____

   mode: _____   mode: _____

   range: _____   range: _____

9. A bag contains nine marbles. Four marbles are blue. Two marbles are green. Two marbles are red. One marble is orange. What is the probability of selecting an orange marble without looking? _____

Lesson 1 Bar Graphs

The **bar graph** shows the number of scooters that were sold at a particular store from January to June of one year.

How many scooters were sold in April?

Locate the top edge of the bar that represents April. Follow this to the left to locate its value on the vertical axis.

In April, ___25___ scooters were sold.

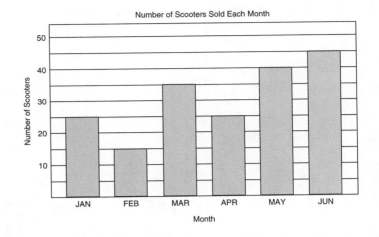

Use the bar graph to answer each question.

1. How many scooters were sold in January? _____

2. How many scooters were sold in March? _____

3. How many scooters were sold in June? _____

4. In which two months were the same number of scooters sold?
    _____

5. How many more scooters were sold in May than in April? _____

6. How many fewer scooters were sold in February than in January? _____

7. What is the minimum number of scooters that need to be sold in July to have more sales than in June? _____

8. During which two consecutive months did the sales increase the most?
    _____

9. During which two consecutive months did the sales decrease the most?
    _____

10. The sales goal for July through December is to sell more scooters than were sold in January through June. What is the minimum number of scooters that need to be sold in July through December to meet the sales goal? _____

Lesson 1 Problem Solving

Use the bar graph to answer each question.

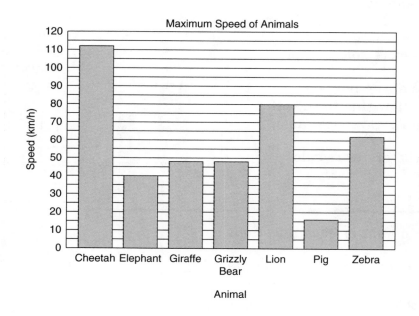

1. What is the maximum speed of a cheetah? _____

2. What is the maximum speed of a giraffe? _____

3. What is the maximum speed of a grizzly bear? _____

4. What is the maximum speed of a pig? _____

5. What is the maximum speed of a zebra? _____

6. How much faster is a lion than an elephant? _____

7. How much slower is a pig than a grizzly bear? _____

8. How much faster is a cheetah than a zebra? _____

9. Which animal(s) is(are) 8 km/h faster than an elephant? _____

10. If an elephant, giraffe, and zebra were racing, which animal would most likely win? _____

Lesson 2 Line Graphs

The **line graph** shows the distance Jordy rode on his bike ride on Saturday.

How many kilometres did Jordy ride by 10:00 A.M.?

Locate the point on the graph that represents 10:00 A.M. Follow this to the left to locate its value on the vertical axis.

By 10:00 A.M., Jordy rode ___15___ km.

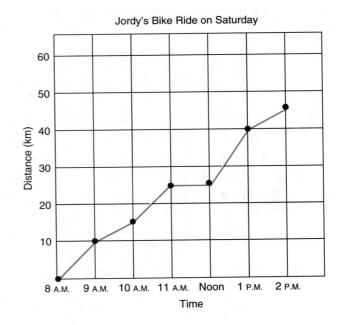

Jordy's Bike Ride on Saturday

Use the line graph of Jordy's bike ride to answer each question.

1. How many kilometres did Jordy ride by 8:00 A.M.? _____

2. How many kilometres did Jordy ride by 11:00 A.M.? _____

3. How many kilometres did Jordy ride by noon? _____

4. How many kilometres did Jordy ride by 2:00 P.M.? _____

5. Between which two consecutive times graphed did Jordy ride the farthest distance? _____

6. Between which two consecutive times graphed did Jordy ride the shortest distance? _____

7. About how many kilometres did Jordy ride by 10:30 A.M.? _____

8. How many more kilometres did Jordy bike between noon and 1:00 P.M. than he biked between 1:00 P.M. and 2:00 P.M.? _____

9. About what time do you think Jordy stopped to eat lunch? _____

10. On Sunday, Jordy biked one-third as far as he did on Saturday. How many kilometres did Jordy bike on Sunday? _____

Lesson 2 Problem Solving

Use the line graph to answer each question.

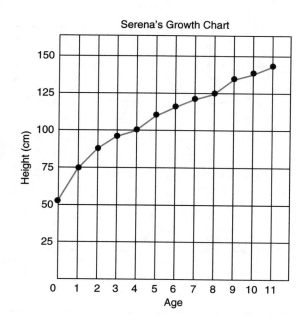

What was Serena's approximate height at the following ages?

1. 0/birth _____ age 2 _____ age 5 _____

2. age 6 _____ age 8 _____ age 11 _____

3. What is the difference in Serena's height at age 4 and her height at age 1? _____

4. What is the difference in Serena's height at age 10 and her height at age 4? _____

5. Between which two consecutive ages did Serena grow the most?
_____

6. Between which two consecutive ages did Serena grow 12.5 cm?
_____

7. If Serena grows 8 cm more by the time she is 12 years old, how tall will she be? _____

8. When Serena was 8 years old she was 40 cm shorter than her mom. How tall is Serena's mom? _____

Lesson 3 Mean

To find the **mean** or average of a set of numbers, add up all the numbers and then divide by the number of addends.

What is the mean of 6, 10, 11, 9?

Add the values.

₁
6
10
11
+9
___
36

Divide by 4, the number of addends.

$$4)\overline{36} \quad \frac{9}{}$$
36
___
0

The mean of 6, 10, 11, 9 is ____9____.

Find the mean of each set of numbers.

	a	*b*
1.	6, 9, 5, 8 _____	13, 21, 10, 16 _____
2.	12, 17, 19, 11, 16 _____	26, 22, 27, 30, 25 _____
3.	42 cm, 35 cm, 33 cm, 41 cm, 39 cm _____	88%, 97%, 92%, 95% _____
4.	$2.48, $2.67, $2.28, $2.45 _____	$1.25, $1.64, $1.38, $1.29 _____

Lesson 3 Problem Solving

Solve each problem.

1. Betsy bought four books at the bookstore. The prices of the books were $4, $5, $8, and $3. What is the mean price of the books? The mean price of the books is _____.	**1.**
2. Keshawn kept track of how long it took him to drive to work every day this week. On Monday, it took 18 min. On Tuesday, it took 22 min. On Wednesday, it took 18 min. On Thursday, it took 21 min. On Friday, it took 26 min. What is the mean amount of time it took Keshawn to drive to work this week? The mean amount of time it took Keshawn to drive to work this week is _____ min.	**2.**
3. On the first three math tests this term, Yoshiyo scored 87%, 95%, and 91%. What is the mean score of Yoshiyo's first three math tests? The mean score of Yoshiyo's first three math tests is _____.	**3.**
4. Ryan and four of his friends measured their heights in centimetres. Their heights were 143 cm, 153 cm, 145 cm, 143 cm, and 155 cm. What is the mean height of Ryan and his friends? The mean height of Ryan and his friends is _____ cm.	**4.**
5. Hussein bought his lunch three days this week at school. He spent $2.50 on Monday, $3.25 on Tuesday, and $2.80 on Thursday. What is the mean amount of money that Hussein spent on lunch this week? The mean amount of money that Hussein spent on lunch this week is _____.	**5.**

Lesson 4 Median, Mode, and Range

The **median** is the middle number of a set of numbers.

The **mode** is the number that appears most often in the set of numbers.

The **range** is the difference between the greatest and least number in the set.

What are the median, mode, and range of 9, 14, 11, 7, 9?

Order the numbers from least to greatest to find the median.

7, 9, 9, 11, 14   The median is ___9___.

The number 9 appears most often.   The mode is ___9___.

Subtract 7 (least) from 14 (greatest) to find the range.

14 − 7 = 7   The range is ___7___.

Find the median, mode, and range of each set of numbers.

a

1. 5, 9, 5, 10, 6   median: _____
                        mode: _____
                        range: _____

2. 15, 17, 11, 13, 15, 10, 14
                        median: _____
                        mode: _____
                        range: _____

3. 87%, 80%, 76%, 84%, 80%
                        median: _____
                        mode: _____
                        range: _____

4. $127, $105, $113, $120, $127
                        median: _____
                        mode: _____
                        range: _____

b

9, 3, 6, 4, 8, 3, 8, 4, 3
                        median: _____
                        mode: _____
                        range: _____

33, 37, 30, 29, 34, 37, 39
                        median: _____
                        mode: _____
                        range: _____

67%, 78%, 85%, 77%, 77%, 73%, 89%
                        median: _____
                        mode: _____
                        range: _____

$58, $65, $44, $63, $44, $65, $44
                        median: _____
                        mode: _____
                        range: _____

Lesson 4 Problem Solving

Answer each question.

1. Shanelle ran five times this week. On Monday, she ran 3 km. On Wednesday, she ran 5 km. On Thursday, she ran 3 km. On Friday, she ran 4 km. On Saturday, she ran 6 km.

   What is the median of the number of kilometres Shanelle ran this week? _____

   What is the mode of the number of kilometres Shanelle ran this week? _____

   What is the range of the number of kilometres Shanelle ran this week? _____

2. David kept track of the amounts of his phone bills over the past 5 months. The amounts of the phone bills were $22, $16, $34, $28, and $16.

   What is the median amount of the phone bills?

   _____

   What is the mode amount of the phone bills?

   _____

   What is the range of the phone bills? _____

3. Enrique had nine math tests all school year. His scores were 78%, 87%, 70%, 76%, 88%, 92%, 73%, 88%, and 90%.

   What is the median score of Enrique's math tests?

   _____

   What is the mode score of Enrique's math tests?

   _____

   What is the range of the scores of Enrique's math tests? _____

4. An electronics store carries five different plasma televisions. The prices of these televisions are $325, $395, $405, $485, and $325.

   What is the median price of televisions at the electronics store? _____

   What is the mode price of televisions at the electronics store? _____

   What is the range of the television prices at the electronics store? _____

1.

2.

3.

4.

Lesson 5 Probabilities

Probability is the chance that something will occur.

What is the probability of spinning a 3?

Spinning a 3 is the favourable outcome. There are 5 possible outcomes.

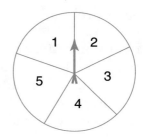

number of favourable outcomes $\longrightarrow$ $\dfrac{1}{5}$
number or possible outcomes $\longrightarrow$

The probability of spinning a 3 is _____ $\dfrac{1}{5}$ _____.

___

You spin the spinner shown at the right. Find the probability of the spinner stopping on

1. Skip Your Turn _____

2. Move Forward 1 _____

3. Move Backward 2 _____

4. Spin Again _____

A bag contains 11 marbles. Five marbles are yellow. Three marbles are red. Two marbles are green. One marble is blue. What is the probability of selecting a marble of the given colour without looking?

| *a* | *b* |

5. red _____   yellow _____

6. blue _____   green _____

7. yellow or blue _____   red or green _____

Lesson 5 Problem Solving

Find each probability.

1. Brittany and Jessica are playing a game in which they roll a number cube each turn. The sides of the number cube are labelled 1–6. On Jessica's turn she is hoping to roll a 2. What is the probability that Jessica will roll a 2?

The probability is _____.

2. Damian has one $20 bill, three $10 bills, and six $5 bills in his wallet. If he selects one bill from his wallet without looking, what is the probability that he will select a $10 bill?

The probability is _____.

3. Luis wrote each of the letters of the alphabet on a separate card. He placed all of these cards face down on the floor. If he selects one card, what is the probability that he will select the card with the letter T?

The probability is _____.

4. Margaret has eight index cards. She writes one letter on each card. When she places the cards side-by-side, they spell her first name. She mixes up the cards and places them face down on her desk. If she selects one of the cards, what is the probability that it will have the letter R or T on it?

The probability is _____.

5. The Whitman family just bought a new dog. They were trying to think of a name for the dog. Their ideas were Fluffy, Baxter, Patch, Babe, and Bailey. They wrote all their ideas on separate pieces of paper and placed them in a bowl. Without looking, they selected the name from the bowl. What is the probability that the name they selected was Patch?

The probability is _____.

1.

2.

3.

4.

5.

CHAPTER 7 PRACTICE TEST
Graphs and Averages

Use the bar graph to answer each question.

1. How many students chose comedy as their favourite movie type? _____

2. How many students chose action as their favourite movie type? _____

3. How many more students chose horror as their favourite movie type than romance? _____

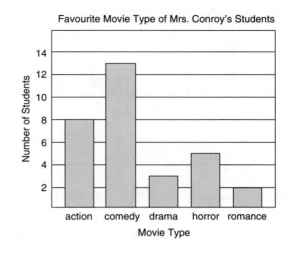

Favourite Movie Type of Mrs. Conroy's Students

Use the line graph to answer each question.

4. How long did it take Nikki to run the first kilometre? _____

5. After 14 min, how far did Nikki run? _____

6. How long did it take Nikki to run 4 km? _____

7. What is the quickest amount of time Nikki ran a kilometre in the race? _____

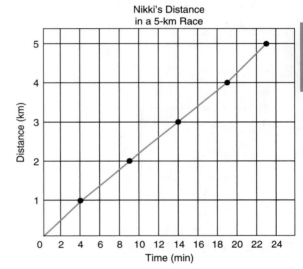

Nikki's Distance in a 5-km Race

Find the mean, median, mode, and range of each set of numbers.

	a	b
8.	78%, 84%, 87%, 95%, 83%, 77%, 84%	$125, $164, $118, $114, $164

       mean: _____   mean: _____

       median: _____   median: _____

       mode: _____   mode: _____

       range: _____   range: _____

9. A bag contains eight marbles. Four marbles are black. Three marbles are white. One marble is red. What is the probability of selecting a white marble without looking? _____

CHAPTER 8   PRETEST
Metric Measurement

Find the length of each line segment to the nearest centimetre (cm).
Then find the length of each line segment to the nearest millimetre (mm).

      a   *b*

1. _____ cm   _____ mm   _____

2. _____ cm   _____ mm   _____

Find the perimeter and the area of each rectangle.

3. *perimeter:* _____ cm

    area: _____ cm^2

4. *perimeter:* _____ mm

    area: _____ mm^2

3 cm   2 cm

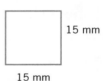

15 mm   15 mm

Complete the following.

           a   *b*

5. 7 cm = _____ mm   28 m = _____ cm

6. 9 m = _____ cm   49 m = _____ mm

7. 8 km = _____ m   16 L = _____ mL

8. 5 kL = _____ L   5 kg = _____ g

9. 2 g = _____ mg   14 cm = _____ mm

10. 40 L = _____ mL   42 m = _____ cm

11. 3 kL = _____ L   35 m = _____ mm

12. 60 kg = _____ g   34 km = _____ m

Lesson 1 Centimetre and Millimetre

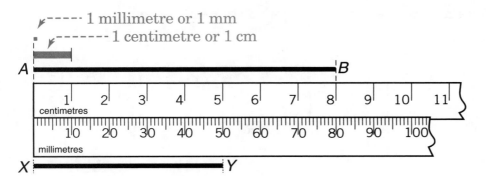

Line segment *AB* is ___8___ cm long.   *XY* is _____ cm long.

Line segment *AB* is ___80___ mm long.   *XY* is _____ mm long.

Find the length of each line segment to the nearest centimetre.
Then find the length of each line segment to the nearest millimetre.

         a   *b*

1. _____ cm   _____ mm

2. _____ cm   _____ mm

3. _____ cm   _____ mm

4. _____ cm   _____ mm

Find the length of each line segment to the nearest millimetre.

5. _____ mm

6. _____ mm

7. _____ mm

8. _____ mm

Draw a line segment for each measurement.

9. 6 cm

10. 45 mm

Lesson 2 Perimeter

The distance around a figure is called its **perimeter.**

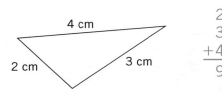

$$\begin{array}{r} 2 \\ 3 \\ +4 \\ \hline 9 \end{array}$$

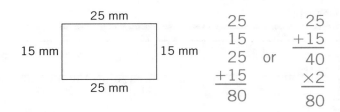

$$\begin{array}{r} 25 \\ 15 \\ 25 \\ +15 \\ \hline 80 \end{array} \quad \text{or} \quad \begin{array}{r} 25 \\ +15 \\ \hline 40 \\ \times 2 \\ \hline 80 \end{array}$$

perimeter: ___9___ cm

perimeter: ___80___ mm

Measure each side in centimetres. Then find the perimeter of each figure.

a	*b*

1. _____ cm

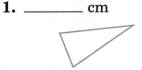

_____ cm

2. _____ cm

_____ cm

Measure each side in millimetres. Then find the perimeter of each figure.

3. _____ mm

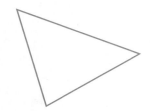

_____ mm

Lesson 3   Metre and Kilometre

A baseball bat is about **1 m** long.

1 metre (m) or 100 cm

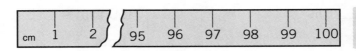

1 m = 100 cm
1 cm = 0.01 m

If you run from goal line to goal line on a football field **10** times, you will run about **1 km.**

1000 m is the same distance as **1** kilometre (km).

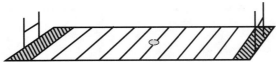

1 km = 1000 m
1 m = 0.001 km

Use a metre stick to find the following to the nearest metre.

a	b
1. length of your room _____ m	width of a door _____ m
2. width of your room _____ m	width of a window_____ m
3. height of a door _____ m	height of a window _____ m

Answer each question.

4. Michelle's height is 105 cm. Is she taller or shorter than 1 m?

She is _____ than 1 m.

4.

5. Are you taller or shorter than 1 m?

I am _____ than 1 m.

5.

6. Roberta wants to swim 1 km. How many metres should she swim?

She should swim _____ m.

6.

7. Sung-Chi ran 1500 m. Leona ran 1 km. Who ran farther? How much farther?

_____ ran _____ m farther.

7.

Lesson 4 Units of Length

Study how to change from one metric unit to another.

$9 \text{ km} = \underline{\quad ? \quad} \text{ m}$ $850 \text{ mm} = \underline{\quad ? \quad} \text{ cm}$

$1 \text{ km} = 1000 \text{ m}$ $10 \text{ mm} = 1 \text{ cm}$

$9 \text{ km} = (9 \times 1000) \text{ m}$ $850 \text{ mm} = (850 \div 10) \text{ cm}$

$9 \text{ km} = \underline{\quad 9000 \quad} \text{ m}$ $850 \text{ mm} = \underline{\quad 85 \quad} \text{ cm}$

Complete the following.

	a		*b*

1. $50 \text{ km} = \underline{\qquad} \text{ m}$ $600 \text{ cm} = \underline{\qquad} \text{ m}$

2. $70 \text{ mm} = \underline{\qquad} \text{ cm}$ $2000 \text{ mm} = \underline{\qquad} \text{ m}$

3. $9 \text{ cm} = \underline{\qquad} \text{ mm}$ $8000 \text{ m} = \underline{\qquad} \text{ km}$

4. $3 \text{ m} = \underline{\qquad} \text{ cm}$ $5000 \text{ cm} = \underline{\qquad} \text{ m}$

5. Ted is 4000 m from school. Susan is 3 km from school. How many metres from school is Susan? Who is farther from school? How much farther?   **5.**

Susan is _____ m from school.

_____ is _____ m farther from school.

6. Maria is 134 cm tall. Su-Lyn is 1300 mm tall. Charles is 141 cm tall. Who is tallest? Who is shortest?   **6.**

_____ is tallest.

_____ is shortest.

7. What is your height in centimetres? In millimetres?   **7.**

I am _____ cm tall.

I am _____ mm tall.

Lesson 5 Area

To find the **area** of a rectangle, multiply the
measure of its length by the measure of its width.

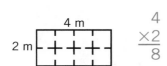

$$\begin{array}{r} 4 \\ \times 2 \\ \hline 8 \end{array}$$

area: ____8____ square metres (m²)

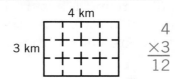

$$\begin{array}{r} 4 \\ \times 3 \\ \hline 12 \end{array}$$

area: ____12____ square kilometres (km²)

Find the area of each rectangle.

	a	*b*	*c*

1. _____ km²   _____ square millimetres (mm²)   _____ m²

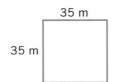

60 mm / 50 mm

7 m / 6 m

2. _____ m²   _____ km²   _____ square centimetres (cm²)

35 m / 35 m   27 km / 20 km   15 cm / 10 cm

	Length	Width	Area
3.	9 km	6 km	_____ km²
4.	18 cm	7 cm	_____ cm²
5.	14 m	10 m	_____ m²
6.	175 mm	25 mm	_____ mm²
7.	152 cm	100 cm	_____ cm²

Lesson 5　Problem Solving

Solve each problem.

1. Find a rectangular room. Measure its length and width to the nearest metre. Find the perimeter of the room. Find the area of the room.

   length: _____ m

   width: _____ m

   perimeter: _____ m

   area: _____ m^2

2. Find a rectangular tabletop or desk. Measure its length and width to the nearest metre. Find the perimeter of the top. Find the area of the top.

   length: _____ m

   width: _____ m

   perimeter: _____ m

   area: _____ m^2

3. Use the front cover of this book. Measure its length and width to the nearest centimetre. Find the perimeter of the cover. Find the area of the front cover.

   perimeter: _____ cm

   area: _____ cm^2

4. Use the rectangle at the right. Find the perimeter of the rectangle. Find the area of the rectangle.

   perimeter: _____ mm

   area: _____ mm^2

35 mm

24 mm

1.

2.

3.

4.

Lesson 6 Volume

To find the **volume** of a rectangular solid, multiply the measure of its length by the measure of its width by the measure of its height.

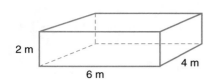

$$\begin{array}{r} 6 \\ \times 4 \\ \hline 24 \\ \times 2 \\ \hline 48 \end{array}$$

volume: ___48___ m³

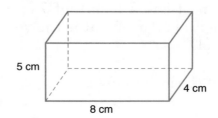

$$\begin{array}{r} 8 \\ \times 4 \\ \hline 32 \\ \times 5 \\ \hline 160 \end{array}$$

volume: ___160___ cm³

Find the volume of each rectangle.

| | *a* | *b* | *c* |

1.

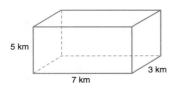
5 km, 7 km, 3 km

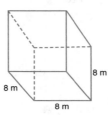
8 m, 8 m, 8 m

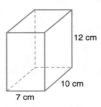
12 cm, 10 cm, 7 cm

_____ km³

_____ m³

_____ cm³

2.

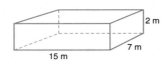
15 m, 7 m, 2 m

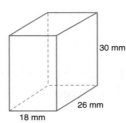
30 mm, 26 mm, 18 mm

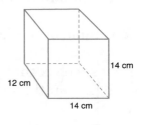
14 cm, 14 cm, 12 cm

_____ m³

_____ mm³

_____ cm³

	Length	*Width*	*Height*	*Volume*
3.	5 m	6 m	7 m	_____ m³
4.	9 km	3 km	8 km	_____ km³
5.	10 cm	13 cm	6 cm	_____ cm³
6.	26 mm	32 mm	15 mm	_____ mm³

Lesson 6 Problem Solving

Solve each problem.

1. A swimming pool has a length of 7 m, a width of 4 m, and a depth of 2 m. What is the volume of the swimming pool?

   The volume of the swimming pool is _____ m^3.

   1.

2. A box of cereal has a length of 21 cm, a width of 6 cm, and a height of 30 cm. What is the volume of the cereal box?

   The volume of the cereal box is _____ cm^3.

   2.

3. A shoebox has a length of 28 cm, a width of 20 cm, and a height of 14 cm. What is the volume of the shoebox?

   The volume of the shoebox is _____ cm^3.

   3.

4. A fish aquarium has a length of 36 cm, a width of 18 cm, and a height of 20 cm. What is the volume of the fish aquarium?

   The volume of the fish aquarium is _____ cm^3.

   4.

5. Find a shoebox that is a rectangular prism. Measure its length, width, and height. Find the volume of the shoebox.

   length: _____

   width: _____

   height: _____

   volume: _____

   5.

Lesson 7 Capacity

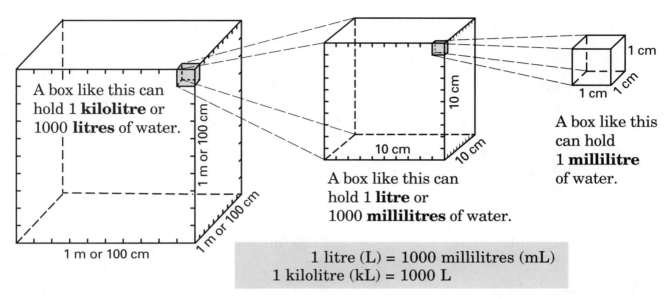

A box like this can hold 1 **kilolitre** or 1000 **litres** of water.

1 m or 100 cm

1 m or 100 cm

1 m or 100 cm

A box like this can hold 1 **litre** or 1000 **millilitres** of water.

10 cm

10 cm

10 cm

A box like this can hold 1 **millilitre** of water.

1 cm

1 cm

1 cm

1 litre (L) = 1000 millilitres (mL)
1 kilolitre (kL) = 1000 L

Solve each problem.

1. A teaspoon holds about 5 mL. A recipe calls for 2 teaspoons of vanilla. How many millilitres is that?

   That is _____ mL.

   1.

2. A litre is slightly more than 4 cups. Do you drink more or less than a litre of milk every day?

   I drink _____ than a litre every day.

   2.

3. To make punch, 8 cups of fruit juice are used. About how many litres would that be?

   That would be _____ L.

   3.

4. Two bathtubs filled with water would be about 1 kL of water. Suppose your family uses 10 tubfuls of water a week. How many kilolitres of water would be used in a week?

   _____ kL would be used in a week.

   4.

5. A tank holds 1000 L. How many kilolitres would it hold?

   It would hold _____ kL.

   5.

Lesson 8 Units of Capacity

19 L = _____?_____ mL   7000 L = _____?_____ kL

   1 L = 1000 mL   1000 L = 1 kL

  19 L = (19×1000) mL   7000 L = $(7000 \div 1000)$ kL

  19 L = __19 000__ mL   7000 L = _____7_____ kL

Complete the following.

          a   *b*

1. 7 L = _____ mL   3000 mL = _____ L

2. 2 kL = _____ L   9000 L = _____ kL

3. 20 L = _____ mL   48 kL = _____ L

4. 4000 mL = _____ L   5000 L = _____ kL

5. Lisa filled an ice-cube tray with water. Do you think she used about 1 mL, 1 L, or 1 kL of water?

  She used 1 _____ of water.

        5.

6. Carlos said he drank 500 mL of milk. Larry said he drank 1 L of milk. Who drank more milk? How many millilitres more?

  _____ drank _____ mL more milk.

        6.

7. The gasoline tank on Mrs. Mohr's truck holds 85 L. It took 27 L of fuel to fill the tank. How much fuel was in the tank before it was filled?

  _____ L were in the tank.

        7.

8. A tank can hold 4000 L of water. There are 3 kL of water in the tank. How many litres of water are needed to fill the tank?

  _____ L are needed.

        8.

Lesson 9   Mass

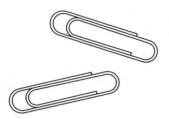

2 paper clips have
a mass of about
1 **gram** (g).

3 math books like yours
have a mass of about
1 **kilogram** (kg).

1 g = 1000 milligrams (mg)
1000 g = 1 kg

Complete the following.

1. About what is the mass of four paper clips?

   Their mass is about _____ g.

   1.

2. A box contains 4000 paper clips. What is the mass of those paper clips?

   Their mass is _____ kg.

   2.

3. One nickel has a mass of about 5 g. A roll of 40 nickels would have a mass of about how many grams?

   It would have a mass of _____ g.

   3.

4. What is the mass of six math books like yours?

   Their mass is _____ kg.

   4.

5. A doctor has 3000 milligrams of medicine. How many grams is that?

   That is _____ g.

   5.

6. A dog has a mass of 17 000 grams. How many kilograms is that?

   That is _____ kg.

   6.

Lesson 10   Units of Mass

6 kg = ___?___ g   5000 mg = ___?___ g

1 kg = 1000 g   1000 mg = 1 g

6 kg = (6 × 1000) g   5000 mg = (5000 ÷ 1000) g

6 kg = __6000__ g   5000 mg = __5__ g

Complete the following.

  a   b

1. 2 kg = _____ g   6 g = _____ mg

2. 9 g = _____ mg   9 kg = _____ g

3. 2000 mg = _____ g   7000 g = _____ kg

4. 3000 g = _____ kg   8000 mg = _____ g

5. A penny has a mass of about 3 g. A dime has a mass of about 2000 mg. Which has the greater mass? How much greater?

A _____ has a mass of about _____ mg more.

5.

6. Emily uses a 4-kg bowling ball. Her father uses a 7-kg bowling ball. How much heavier is her father's bowling ball?

It is _____ kg heavier.

6.

7. A loaf of bread has a mass of 454 grams. What is the mass of 3 loaves of bread?

Their mass is _____ g.

7.

8. John's mass is 34 000 grams. Judy's mass is 39 kg. Whose mass is more? How much more?

_____'s mass is _____ kg more.

8.

CHAPTER 8   PRACTICE TEST

Find the length of each line segment to the nearest centimetre.
Then find the length of each line segment to the nearest millimetre.

	a	*b*

1. _____ cm   _____ mm   ━━━━━━━━━━━━━

2. _____ cm   _____ mm   ━━━━━━━━━━━━━━━━━

Find the perimeter and the area of each rectangle.

3. *perimeter:* _____ m

   area: _____ m²

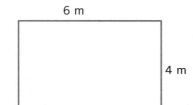
6 m

4 m

4. *perimeter:* _____ mm

   area: _____ mm²

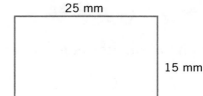
25 mm

15 mm

Find the volume.

	Length	*Width*	*Height*	*Volume*
5.	9 cm	12 cm	6 cm	_____ cm³
6.	2 m	7 m	36 m	_____ m³

Complete the following.

	a	*b*

7. 5 cm = _____ mm   2000 m = _____ km

8. 700 cm = _____ m   300 mm = _____ cm

9. 6 km = _____ m   3 m = _____ cm

10. 4 kL = _____ L   3000 mL = _____ L

CHAPTER 8

CHAPTER 9   PRETEST
More Metric Measurement

Complete.

	a		*b*

1. 4 m = _____ cm   5 m = _____ cm

2. 200 cm = _____ m   6 km = _____ m

3. 5 km = _____ m   3 m = _____ mm

4. 1 km = _____ m   20 m = _____ cm

5. 6000 mL = _____ L   3 L = _____ mL

6. 5000 L = _____ kL   10 L = _____ mL

7. 1000 g = _____ kg   3 kg = _____ g

Find the perimeter of each figure.

           a   *b*   *c*

8. _____ m   _____ cm   _____ km

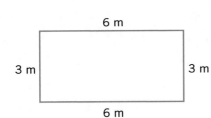

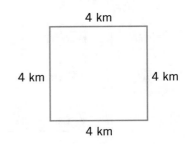

Find the area of each rectangle.

9. _____ m^2 _____ cm^2 _____ mm^2

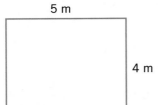

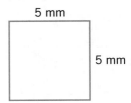

Lesson 1 Units of Length

| 1 m = 100 cm |
| 1 m = 1000 mm |

| 1 km = 1000 m |

200 cm = ___?___ m

100 cm = 1 m

200 cm = (200 ÷ 100) m

200 cm = ___2___ m

3 km = ___?___ m

1 km = 1000 m

3 km = (3 × 1000) or 3000 m

3 km = _____ m

Complete the following.

	a	*b*
1.	6 m = _____ cm	3 m = _____ mm
2.	2 m = _____ mm	6 m = _____ cm
3.	3 km = _____ m	4 km = _____ m
4.	400 cm = _____ m	7 m = _____ mm
5.	4000 mm = _____ m	4 m = _____ cm
6.	300 cm = _____ m	32 km = _____ m

7. Becky threw the ball 8 m. Zachary threw the ball 840 cm. How many centimetres did each person throw the ball? Who threw it farther? How much farther?

Becky threw the ball _____ cm.

Zachary threw the ball _____ cm.

_____ threw the ball _____ cm farther.

Lesson 2 Perimeter

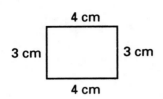

4 cm

3 cm   3 cm

4 cm

$$\begin{array}{c}3\\4\\3\\+4\\\hline 14\end{array}$$ or $$\begin{array}{c}3\\+4\\\hline 7\\\times 2\\\hline 14\end{array}$$

perimeter: ____14____ cm

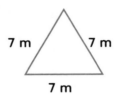

7 m

5 m   3 m

3 m   4 m

$$\begin{array}{c}5\\7\\3\\4\\+3\\\hline 22\end{array}$$

perimeter: _____ m

Find the perimeter of each figure.

       a   *b*

1. _____ cm

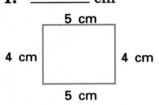

5 cm

4 cm   4 cm

5 cm

_____ m

7 m   7 m

7 m

2. _____ m

4 m

5 m   3 m

_____ mm

3 mm

4 mm   3 mm

2 mm

3. _____ cm

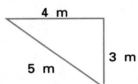

Each side
is 1 cm
long.

_____ cm

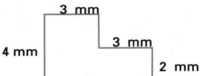

3 cm

4 cm   4 cm

5 cm

4. _____ m

3 m

3 m   3 m

3 m

_____ km

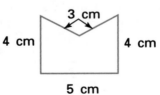

2 km

4 km   3 km

2 km

6 km

Lesson 3 Area

3 cm

2 cm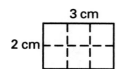

$$\begin{array}{r} 3 \\ \times 2 \\ \hline 6 \end{array}$$

area: ___6___ cm²

3 m

3 m

$$\begin{array}{r} 3 \\ \times 3 \\ \hline 9 \end{array}$$

area: ___9___ m²

Find the area of each rectangle.

a   b

1. _____ cm²   _____ m²

5 cm

2 cm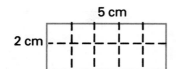

7 m

6 m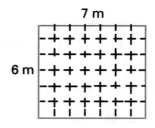

2. _____ km²   _____ mm²

8 km

8 km

2 mm

2 mm

	Length	Width	Area
3.	8 m	5 m	_____ m²
4.	12 cm	8 cm	_____ cm²
5.	142 m	57 m	_____ m²
6.	36 km	12 km	_____ km²
7.	18 mm	15 mm	_____ mm²

CHAPTER 9

Lesson 3 Problem Solving

Solve each problem.

1. A garden has the shape of a rectangle. It is 24 m long and 10 m wide. What is the perimeter of the garden?

   The perimeter is _____ m.

2. A baseball diamond is a square with each side 27 m long. Find the perimeter and the area of the diamond.

   The perimeter is _____ m.

   The area is _____ m^2.

3. A square-shaped lot is 125 m on each side. What is the perimeter of the lot? What is the area?

   The perimeter is _____ m.

   The area is _____ m^2.

4. Find the perimeter and the area of the following figure.

   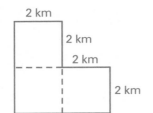

   The perimeter is _____ km.

   The area is _____ km^2.

5. Use the front cover of this book. Measure its length and its width to the nearest centimetre. Find the perimeter of the cover. Find the area of the cover.

   The length of the cover is _____ cm.

   The width of the cover is _____ cm.

   The perimeter of the cover is _____ cm.

   The area of the cover is _____ cm^2.

1.	2.
3.	**4.**
5.	

Lesson 4 Volume

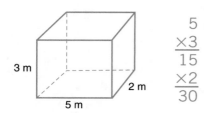

3 m

2 m

5 m

$$\begin{array}{r} 5 \\ \times 3 \\ \hline 15 \\ \times 2 \\ \hline 30 \end{array}$$

volume: ___30___ m³

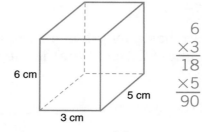

6 cm

5 cm

3 cm

$$\begin{array}{r} 6 \\ \times 3 \\ \hline 18 \\ \times 5 \\ \hline 90 \end{array}$$

volume: ___90___ cm³

Find the volume of each rectangular solid.

| *a* | *b* | *c* |

1.

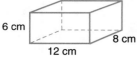

2 cm

4 cm

8 cm

_____ cm³

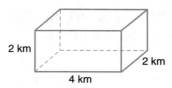

2 km

2 km

4 km

_____ km³

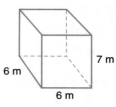

7 m

6 m

6 m

_____ m³

2.

6 cm

8 cm

12 cm

_____ cm³

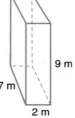

9 m

7 m

2 m

_____ m³

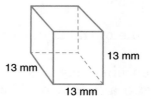

13 mm

13 mm

13 mm

_____ mm³

	Length	Width	Height	Volume
3.	4 km	8 km	3 km	_____ km³
4.	7 cm	9 cm	11 cm	_____ cm³
5.	8 m	15 m	5 m	_____ m³
6.	18 m	12 m	10 m	_____ m³
7.	10 mm	15 mm	6 mm	_____ mm³

CHAPTER 9

Lesson 4 Problem Solving

Solve each problem.

1. A box of crackers has a length of 18 cm, a width of
   8 cm, and a height of 23 cm. What is the volume of
   the cracker box?

   The volume of the cracker box is _____ cm³.

2. A swimming pool has a length of 5 m, a width of
   3 m, and a depth of 1 m. What is the volume of the
   swimming pool?

   The volume of the swimming pool is _____ m³.

3. The bed of a truck has a length of 3 m, a width of
   2 m, and a height of 1 m. What is the volume of the
   bed of the truck?

   The volume of the bed of the truck is _____ m³.

4. A fish aquarium has a length of 63 cm, a width of
   30 cm, and a height of 28 cm. What is the volume
   of the aquarium?

   The volume of the aquarium is _____ cm³.

5. A kitchen sink has a length of 38 cm, a width of
   36 cm, and a height of 23 cm. What is the volume
   of the kitchen sink?

   The volume of the kitchen sink is _____ cm³.

6. Find a cereal box that is a rectangular prism.
   Measure its length, width, and height. Find the
   volume of the cereal box.

   length: _____

   width: _____

   height: _____

   volume: _____

1.

2.

3.

4.

5.

6.

Lesson 5 Capacity

$$1 \text{ kL} = 1000 \text{ L}$$
$$1 \text{ L} = 1000 \text{ mL}$$

6 L = ___?___ mL
1 L = 1000 mL
6 L = (6 × 1000) mL

6 L = __6000__ mL

2 kL = ___?___ L
1 kL = 1000 L
2 kL = (2 × 1000) L

2 kL = _____ L

Complete the following.

	a	*b*
1.	8000 mL = _____ L	5 L = _____ mL
2.	8000 L = _____ kL	16 000 L = _____ kL
3.	16 L = _____ mL	3 L = _____ mL
4.	5 L = _____ mL	6 kL = _____ L
5.	15 kL = _____ L	7 L = _____ mL

6. Alex bought 6 L of milk. He is going to give 1 L of milk to each person. How many people can he serve?

   He can serve _____ people.

7. Mindy bought 6000 mL of fruit juice. Sara bought 5 L of fruit juice. How many total litres of fruit juice did each person buy? Who bought more? How many litres more?

   Mindy bought _____ L.

   Sara bought _____ L.

   _____ bought _____ L more.

6.

7.

Lesson 5 Problem Solving

Solve each problem.

1. A fruit-drink recipe calls for 4 L of water. How many millilitres of water is this?

It is _____ mL of water.

2. Ross counted 7 L of milk and 3000 mL of milk in the cooler. How many total litres of milk was this? How many total millilitres of milk was this?

It was _____ L of milk.

It was _____ mL of milk.

3. Bri has 12 L of juice. How many people can she serve at 200 mL per person? How many can she serve at 400 mL per person?

She can serve _____ people at 200 mL each.

She can serve _____ people at 400 mL each.

4. Gloria filled her pool with 8 kL of water. How many litres was that?

It was _____ L of water.

5. It took 15 L of tea to fill sixty china teacups. How many millilitres of tea is that?

It is _____ mL of tea.

6. Jamal poured 3 L of water and 1000 mL of cleaner into a bucket. How many litres is that?

It is _____ L of water and cleaner.

7. Rob needs 11 L of milk to make hot cocoa for his friends. How many millilitres of milk should he buy?

Rob should buy _____ mL of milk.

1.

2.

3.

4.

5.

6.

7.

Lesson 6 Mass

| 1 kg = 1000 g |
| 1 g = 1000 mg |

3 kg = ___?___ g   2000 mg = ___?___ g

   1 kg = 1000 g   1000 mg = 1 g

   3 kg = (3 × 1000) g   2000 mg = (2000 ÷ 1000) g

3 kg = __3000__ g   2000 mg = _____ 2 g

Complete the following.

        a   *b*

1. 5 kg = _____ g   16 000 mg = _____ g

2. 9000 g = _____ kg   3 kg = _____ g

3. 6 g = _____ mg   6 g = _____ mg

4. 5000 mg = _____ g   5 kg = _____ g

5. 6000 g = _____ kg   11 g = _____ mg

6. Anna's cat's mass is 4 kg. The cat's collar has a mass of 85 g. How many grams is the cat's mass when it is wearing its collar?

    The cat's mass is _____ g with its collar.

6.

7. Juyong took a 2-kg stack of letters to the post office. Each of the 20 letters had the same mass. How many grams was each letter's mass?

    Each letter's mass was _____ g.

7.

Lesson 6 Problem Solving

Solve each problem.

1. Lauren and John have 2 kg of hamburger. How many grams do they have?

   They have _____ g.

   1. _____

2. How many 100-g hamburgers can be made from the meat in problem **1**?

   _____ 100-g hamburgers can be made.

   2. _____

3. How many 200-g hamburgers can be made from the meat in problem **1**?

   _____ 200-g hamburgers can be made.

   3. _____

4. How many 250-g hamburgers can be made from the meat in problem **1**?

   _____ 250-g hamburgers can be made.

   4. _____

5. The candy shop sells 100-g squares of fudge. Teresa buys 1 kg of fudge. How many squares of fudge does Teresa buy?

   Teresa buys _____ squares of fudge.

   5. _____

6. Paul has 24 marbles in a bag. Each marble weighs 80 g. If he adds one more marble to his bag, how much will the bag's mass be in kilograms?

   The bag's mass will be _____ kg.

   6. _____

7. Ramon wants to carry a backpack when he hikes. He has packed a 500 g bag of granola, a map that has a mass of 200 g, and some apples that has a mass of 500 g. How many grams of these supplies has Ramon packed in his backpack?

   Ramon has packed _____ g in his backpack.

   7. _____

CHAPTER 9   PRACTICE TEST
More Metric Measurement

Complete the following.

	a	*b*

1. 7 L = _____ mL   9 m = _____ cm

2. 8000 mL = _____ L   300 cm = _____ m

3. 7000 L = _____ kL   10 km = _____ m

4. 5 L = _____ mL   5 kL = _____ L

5. 7 L = _____ mL   6 L = _____ mL

Find the perimeter of each figure below.

　　　　　　　a　　　　　　　　　　　*b*　　　　　　　　　　　*c*

6.

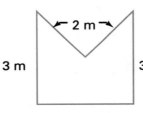

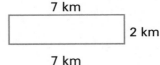

_____ cm   _____ m   _____ km

Find the area of each rectangle below.

7.

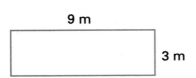

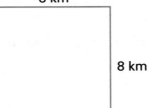

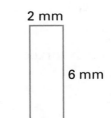

_____ m²   _____ km²   _____ mm²

Find the volume.

	Length	Width	Height	Volume
8.	16 cm	4 cm	9 cm	_____ cm³
9.	11 m	26 m	3 m	_____ m³

CHAPTER 10 PRETEST
Fractions

Write the fraction that tells how much of each figure is coloured.

a	b	c	d

1.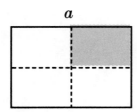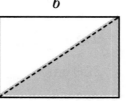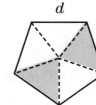

_____   _____   _____   _____

Change each fraction to simplest form.

a	b	c

2. $\dfrac{4}{6}$ $\dfrac{8}{16}$ $\dfrac{15}{20}$

Rename as mixed numerals.

3. $\dfrac{7}{6}$ $\dfrac{8}{3}$ $\dfrac{17}{5}$

Change each mixed numeral to an improper fraction.

4. $3\dfrac{1}{4}$ $6\dfrac{1}{2}$ $3\dfrac{5}{6}$

Change each of the following to simplest form.

5. $1\dfrac{6}{8}$ $\dfrac{10}{3}$ $4\dfrac{5}{2}$

Lesson 1   Writing Fractions

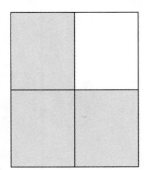

The figure is separated into 4 parts. Each part is the same size. 3 of the 4 parts are blue.

$\frac{3}{4}$ (read *three fourths*) of the figure is blue.

_____ of the 4 parts is not coloured.

_____ of the figure is not coloured.

$\frac{3}{4}$ and $\frac{1}{4}$ are **fractions.**

On the first ___ beneath each figure, write the fraction that tells how much of the figure is blue. On the second ___ , write the fraction that tells how much of the figure is not coloured.

| | *a* | *b* | *c* | *d* |

1.

_____   _____   _____   _____

_____   _____   _____   _____

2.

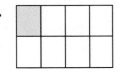   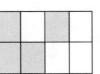   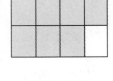

_____   _____   _____   _____

_____   _____   _____   _____

3.

_____   _____   _____   _____

_____   _____   _____   _____

4.

_____   _____   _____   _____

_____   _____   _____   _____

CHAPTER 10

Lesson 2 Writing Fractions

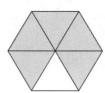

$\frac{5}{6}$ of the figure is coloured.

$\frac{5}{6}$ ⟵——— numerator
⟵——— denominator

$\frac{1}{6}$ of the figure is not coloured.

The denominator of $\frac{1}{6}$ is _____. The numerator of $\frac{1}{6}$ is _____.

Write a fraction for each of the following.

	a		*b*	
1.	three fifths	_____	numerator 2, denominator 3	_____
2.	four sevenths	_____	denominator 5, numerator 4	_____
3.	five eighths	_____	denominator 4, numerator 3	_____
4.	one fifth	_____	numerator 1, denominator 6	_____
5.	two ninths	_____	denominator 9, numerator 5	_____

Colour each figure as directed.

	a	*b*	*c*	*d*
6.	colour $\frac{1}{2}$	colour $\frac{1}{4}$	colour $\frac{2}{3}$	colour $\frac{1}{3}$

7.

colour $\frac{2}{6}$ 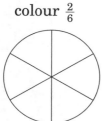 colour $\frac{1}{3}$  colour $\frac{4}{8}$ 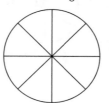 colour $\frac{1}{2}$

Lesson 3 Prime and Composite

A **factor** is a number that divides evenly (no remainder) into a given number.

A **prime number** is a number greater than 1 that has only 1 and itself as factors.

For example, 3 is a prime number because 1 and 3 are its only factors.

A **composite number** is a number that has more than two factors.

For example, 10 is a composite number because 1, 2, 5, and 10 are its factors.

List the factors of each number.

	a		b	
1.	5	_____	8	_____
2.	12	_____	11	_____
3.	6	_____	22	_____
4.	7	_____	13	_____
5.	15	_____	24	_____
6.	20	_____	9	_____

Identify each number as prime or composite.

	a		b	
7.	8	_____	17	_____
8.	14	_____	9	_____
9.	7	_____	11	_____
10.	12	_____	33	_____
11.	31	_____	27	_____
12.	25	_____	19	_____

Lesson 4   Greatest Common Factor

The **greatest common factor** of two or more numbers is the largest factor they have in common.

What is the greatest common factor of 12 and 18?

List all the factors of both numbers.

12: ①, ②, ③, 4, ⑥, 12

18: ①, ②, ③, ⑥, 9, 18

Circle all their common factors.

The greatest common factor of 12 and 18 is __6__ .

List the common factors of each set of numbers.

	a		b

1. 8 and 14   15 and 30

_____   _____

2. 9 and 21   16 and 36

_____   _____

Find the greatest common factor of each set of numbers.

3. 15 and 20   _____   16 and 24   _____

4. 21 and 27   _____   20 and 28   _____

5. 36 and 48   _____   40 and 56   _____

6. 12, 24, and 36   _____   18, 30, and 42   _____

Lesson 5 Fractions in Simplest Form

A fraction is in simplest form when the only whole number
that will divide both the numerator and the denominator is 1.

$\dfrac{12}{18} = \dfrac{12 \div 6}{18 \div 6}$ $\longleftarrow$ Divide both the numerator $\longrightarrow$ $\dfrac{12}{18} = \dfrac{12 \div 2}{18 \div 2}$

$= \dfrac{2}{3}$ and the denominator by the same number. $= \dfrac{6}{9}$ $\longleftarrow$ This fraction is not in simplest form, so

$= \dfrac{6 \div 3}{9 \div 3}$ continue dividing the numerator and the denominator until the

$= \dfrac{2}{3}$ fraction is in simplest form.

Change each fraction to simplest form.

	a	b	c
1.	$\dfrac{4}{6}$	$\dfrac{4}{16}$	$\dfrac{12}{15}$
2.	$\dfrac{12}{32}$	$\dfrac{8}{10}$	$\dfrac{15}{20}$
3.	$\dfrac{14}{16}$	$\dfrac{6}{8}$	$\dfrac{10}{16}$
4.	$\dfrac{6}{10}$	$\dfrac{3}{24}$	$\dfrac{8}{16}$
5.	$\dfrac{14}{21}$	$\dfrac{10}{12}$	$\dfrac{12}{16}$

CHAPTER 10

Lesson 5 Fractions in Simplest Form

Change each fraction to simplest form.

	a	*b*	*c*
1.	$\dfrac{4}{8}$	$\dfrac{3}{6}$	$\dfrac{2}{4}$
2.	$\dfrac{5}{10}$	$\dfrac{3}{15}$	$\dfrac{4}{20}$
3.	$\dfrac{4}{24}$	$\dfrac{8}{12}$	$\dfrac{6}{9}$
4.	$\dfrac{6}{21}$	$\dfrac{10}{25}$	$\dfrac{4}{12}$
5.	$\dfrac{12}{30}$	$\dfrac{12}{28}$	$\dfrac{16}{20}$
6.	$\dfrac{20}{24}$	$\dfrac{20}{36}$	$\dfrac{42}{49}$
7.	$\dfrac{21}{35}$	$\dfrac{15}{18}$	$\dfrac{24}{30}$
8.	$\dfrac{16}{24}$	$\dfrac{15}{35}$	$\dfrac{24}{32}$

Lesson 6 Improper Fractions

$\frac{17}{5}$ means $17 \div 5$ or $5\overline{)17}$

$\begin{array}{r} 3\frac{2}{5} \\ 5\overline{)17} \\ 15 \\ \hline 2 \end{array} \rightarrow 2 \div 5 = \frac{2}{5}$

$\frac{17}{5} = 3\frac{2}{5}$

$3\frac{2}{5}$ is a **mixed numeral.** It means $3 + \frac{2}{5}$.

Rename as mixed numerals.

	a	b	c
1.	$\frac{9}{4}$	$\frac{6}{5}$	$\frac{9}{8}$
2.	$\frac{8}{3}$	$\frac{9}{5}$	$\frac{7}{3}$
3.	$\frac{7}{4}$	$\frac{29}{6}$	$\frac{14}{3}$
4.	$\frac{15}{7}$	$\frac{12}{5}$	$\frac{19}{9}$
5.	$\frac{22}{7}$	$\frac{19}{2}$	$\frac{27}{5}$
6.	$\frac{35}{8}$	$\frac{43}{7}$	$\frac{55}{6}$

CHAPTER 10

Lesson 7   Renaming Numbers

Study how to change a mixed numeral to an improper fraction.

$$2\frac{1}{4} = \frac{(4 \times 2) + 1}{4}$$

Multiply the whole number by the denominator and add the numerator. **Use the same denominator.**

$$4\frac{2}{3} = \frac{(3 \times 4) + 2}{3}$$

$$= \frac{8 + 1}{4}$$

$$= \frac{9}{4}$$

$$= \frac{12 + 2}{3}$$

$$= \frac{14}{3}$$

Change each mixed numeral to an improper fraction.

	a	*b*	*c*
1.	$2\frac{1}{3}$	$3\frac{1}{2}$	$4\frac{3}{4}$
2.	$6\frac{4}{5}$	$3\frac{3}{8}$	$2\frac{5}{9}$
3.	$2\frac{1}{5}$	$1\frac{2}{7}$	$5\frac{3}{7}$
4.	$6\frac{5}{12}$	$7\frac{3}{10}$	$8\frac{6}{15}$

Lesson 8 Mixed Numerals

A mixed numeral is in simplest form when the fraction is in simplest form and names a number less than 1.

$$5\frac{4}{8} = 5 + \frac{4}{8}$$

$$= 5 + \frac{4 \div 4}{8 \div 4}$$

$$= 5 + \frac{1}{2}$$

$$= 5\frac{1}{2}$$

$$1\frac{18}{8} = 1 + \frac{18}{8}$$

$$= 1 + \frac{18 \div 2}{8 \div 2}$$

$$= 1 + \frac{9}{4}$$

$$\frac{9}{4} = 9 \div 4 = 2$$

$$= 1 + 2\frac{1}{2}$$

$$= 3\frac{1}{4}$$

Change each mixed numeral to simplest form.

	a	*b*	*c*
1.	$3\frac{4}{6}$	$1\frac{4}{8}$	$2\frac{6}{8}$
2.	$4\frac{3}{12}$	$2\frac{6}{16}$	$1\frac{10}{12}$
3.	$1\frac{7}{5}$	$3\frac{9}{6}$	$2\frac{8}{6}$
4.	$1\frac{12}{10}$	$2\frac{15}{10}$	$4\frac{14}{6}$

CHAPTER 10

Lesson 9 Simplest Form

Change each fraction to simplest form.

	a	*b*	*c*
1.	$\dfrac{6}{14}$	$\dfrac{12}{27}$	$\dfrac{15}{25}$
2.	$\dfrac{4}{12}$	$\dfrac{28}{32}$	$\dfrac{15}{21}$

Change each of the following to a mixed numeral in simplest form.

3.	$\dfrac{9}{5}$	$\dfrac{8}{3}$	$\dfrac{12}{7}$
4.	$\dfrac{12}{8}$	$\dfrac{16}{6}$	$\dfrac{25}{15}$
5.	$1\dfrac{8}{10}$	$2\dfrac{7}{21}$	$3\dfrac{9}{15}$
6.	$4\dfrac{12}{14}$	$5\dfrac{8}{12}$	$2\dfrac{12}{16}$

CHAPTER 10 PRACTICE TEST
Fractions

Change each fraction to simplest form.

	a	b	c	d
1.	$\dfrac{4}{8}$	$\dfrac{5}{10}$	$\dfrac{6}{9}$	$\dfrac{3}{6}$
2.	$\dfrac{10}{15}$	$\dfrac{6}{8}$	$\dfrac{12}{18}$	$\dfrac{9}{12}$

Rename as mixed numerals.

3.	$\dfrac{5}{2}$	$\dfrac{7}{5}$	$\dfrac{9}{4}$	$\dfrac{16}{3}$

Change each mixed numeral to a fraction.

4.	$1\dfrac{1}{2}$	$1\dfrac{7}{8}$	$4\dfrac{2}{3}$	$5\dfrac{5}{6}$

Change each of the following to simplest form.

5.	$1\dfrac{8}{10}$	$\dfrac{18}{8}$	$1\dfrac{7}{3}$	$5\dfrac{12}{8}$

CHAPTER 11 PRETEST
Multiplication of Fractions

Write each answer in simplest form.

	a	*b*	*c*
1.	$\dfrac{3}{7} \times \dfrac{2}{5}$	$\dfrac{3}{4} \times \dfrac{7}{8}$	$\dfrac{4}{5} \times \dfrac{4}{5}$
2.	$\dfrac{2}{3} \times \dfrac{7}{8}$	$\dfrac{5}{9} \times \dfrac{3}{5}$	$\dfrac{9}{10} \times \dfrac{5}{12}$
3.	$4 \times \dfrac{2}{3}$	$3 \times \dfrac{5}{6}$	$\dfrac{5}{8} \times 10$
4.	$3\dfrac{1}{5} \times 4$	$2\dfrac{1}{4} \times 8$	$6 \times 1\dfrac{5}{6}$
5.	$2\dfrac{1}{2} \times 2\dfrac{1}{3}$	$2\dfrac{1}{4} \times 1\dfrac{1}{5}$	$1\dfrac{1}{8} \times 3\dfrac{1}{3}$

Lesson 1 Multiplication (using diagrams)

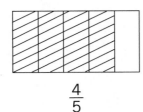

$\frac{4}{5}$

$\frac{2}{3}$ {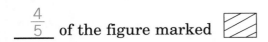

$\frac{4}{5}$

$\underline{5}$ parts in all.

$\underline{4}$ parts marked ▨

$\underline{\frac{4}{5}}$ of the figure marked ▨

$\underline{15}$ parts in all.

$\underline{}$ parts marked

$\underline{}$ of the figure marked ▨

$\frac{2}{3}$ of $\frac{4}{5}$ = $\frac{8}{15}$

Complete the following.

1.   *a*

$\frac{1}{4}$ $\frac{1}{2}$ of $\frac{1}{4}$

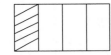   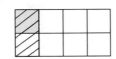

$\frac{1}{2}$ of $\frac{1}{4}$ = _____

b

$\frac{1}{2}$ $\frac{1}{2}$ of $\frac{1}{2}$

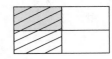

$\frac{1}{2}$ of $\frac{1}{2}$ = _____

---

2. $\frac{1}{2}$ $\frac{1}{3}$ of $\frac{1}{2}$

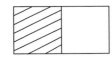   

$\frac{1}{3}$ of $\frac{1}{2}$ = _____

$\frac{1}{3}$ $\frac{1}{2}$ of $\frac{1}{3}$

    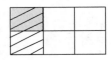

$\frac{1}{2}$ of $\frac{1}{3}$ = _____

---

3. $\frac{1}{5}$ $\frac{1}{2}$ of $\frac{1}{5}$

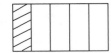   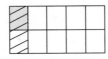

$\frac{1}{2}$ of $\frac{1}{5}$ = _____

$\frac{3}{5}$ $\frac{1}{2}$ of $\frac{3}{5}$

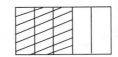   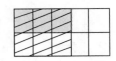

$\frac{1}{2}$ of $\frac{3}{5}$ = _____

CHAPTER 11

Lesson 2 Multiplication

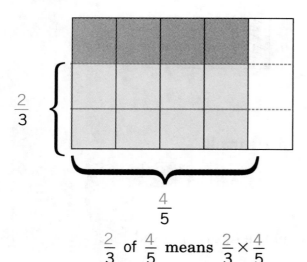

$\frac{2}{3}$

$\frac{4}{5}$

$\frac{2}{3}$ of $\frac{4}{5}$ means $\frac{2}{3} \times \frac{4}{5}$

Multiply numerators.

$$\frac{2}{3} \times \frac{4}{5} = \frac{2 \times 4}{3 \times 5} = \frac{8}{15}$$

Multiply denominators.

Multiply as shown.

	a	b	c
1.	$\frac{1}{4} \times \frac{3}{5} = \frac{1 \times 3}{4 \times 5}$ $= \frac{3}{20}$	$\frac{2}{3} \times \frac{1}{5}$	$\frac{1}{6} \times \frac{5}{8}$
2.	$\frac{3}{7} \times \frac{1}{4}$	$\frac{5}{9} \times \frac{1}{2}$	$\frac{6}{7} \times \frac{2}{5}$
3.	$\frac{4}{5} \times \frac{2}{3}$	$\frac{7}{8} \times \frac{1}{6}$	$\frac{1}{5} \times \frac{2}{3}$
4.	$\frac{2}{5} \times \frac{1}{7}$	$\frac{5}{6} \times \frac{1}{2}$	$\frac{2}{3} \times \frac{5}{7}$
5.	$\frac{2}{3} \times \frac{2}{5}$	$\frac{5}{8} \times \frac{3}{4}$	$\frac{2}{5} \times \frac{1}{3}$

Lesson 3 Multiplication

$$\frac{4}{5} \times \frac{1}{2} = \frac{4 \times 1}{5 \times 2}$$ ⟵— Multiply the numerators. —⟶ $$\frac{3}{10} \times \frac{5}{6} = \frac{3 \times 5}{10 \times 6}$$

⟵— **Multiply the denominators.**—⟶

$$= \frac{4}{10}$$

$$= \frac{15}{60}$$

$$= \frac{2}{5}$$ ⟵——— If necessary, change the ———⟶ $$= \frac{1}{4}$$

answer to simplest form.

Write each answer in simplest form.

	a	*b*	*c*
1.	$\frac{5}{7} \times \frac{1}{4}$	$\frac{3}{5} \times \frac{1}{2}$	$\frac{7}{8} \times \frac{3}{4}$
2.	$\frac{3}{7} \times \frac{2}{5}$	$\frac{1}{4} \times \frac{7}{8}$	$\frac{3}{5} \times \frac{4}{9}$
3.	$\frac{4}{7} \times \frac{3}{8}$	$\frac{9}{10} \times \frac{5}{6}$	$\frac{5}{9} \times \frac{6}{10}$
4.	$\frac{8}{15} \times \frac{5}{12}$	$\frac{5}{12} \times \frac{16}{25}$	$\frac{4}{9} \times \frac{9}{14}$
5.	$\frac{6}{7} \times \frac{2}{3}$	$\frac{7}{8} \times \frac{11}{12}$	$\frac{3}{10} \times \frac{7}{8}$

CHAPTER 11

Lesson 3 Problem Solving

Solve. Write each answer in simplest form.

1. Ontario has $\frac{1}{4}$ of Canada's fresh water. Manitoba has $\frac{1}{2}$ of the fresh water that Ontario does. How much of Canada's fresh water does Manitoba have?

Manitoba has _____ of Canada's fresh water.

1.

2. Virginia Falls in the Northwest Territories is $\frac{3}{4}$ the height of Bridal Veil Falls in British Columbia. Bridal Veil Falls is $\frac{2}{3}$ the height of Panther Falls in Alberta. What fraction of the height of Panther Falls is Virginia Falls?

Virginia Falls is _____ the height of Panther Falls.

2.

3. Marla bought a carton of milk. She drank $\frac{1}{2}$ of it. Her brother drank $\frac{1}{4}$ of what was left. How much milk did he drink?

He drank _____ carton.

3.

4. Hakeem brought $\frac{3}{4}$ round of cheese. He ate $\frac{1}{3}$ of it. How much cheese did he eat?

He ate _____ round.

4.

5. Five sixths of a room is now painted. Carlos did $\frac{2}{5}$ of the painting. How much of the room did he paint?

He painted _____ of the room.

5.

6. The lawn is $\frac{1}{2}$ mowed. Melinda did $\frac{2}{3}$ of the mowing. How much of the lawn did she mow?

She mowed _____ of the lawn.

6.

7. $\frac{5}{6}$ of a carton of eggs has been used. Eric used $\frac{1}{5}$ of those eggs. How much of a carton did Eric use?

Eric used _____ of a carton.

7.

Lesson 4 Multiplication (by whole numbers)

$$4 \times \frac{2}{5} = \frac{4}{1} \times \frac{2}{5}$$

$$= \frac{4 \times 2}{1 \times 5}$$

$$= \frac{8}{5}$$

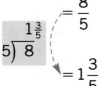

$$= 1\frac{3}{5}$$

Name the whole number as a fraction.

Multiply the fractions.

Change the answer to simplest form.

$$\frac{5}{8} \times 6 = \frac{5}{8} \times \frac{6}{1}$$

$$= \frac{5 \times 6}{8 \times 1}$$

$$= \frac{30}{8}$$

$$8\overline{)30} \quad 3\frac{3}{4}$$

$$= 3\frac{3}{4}$$

Write each answer in simplest form.

	a	*b*	*c*
1.	$5 \times \frac{3}{7}$	$9 \times \frac{7}{8}$	$7 \times \frac{5}{6}$
2.	$\frac{2}{3} \times 5$	$\frac{7}{8} \times 9$	$\frac{4}{5} \times 12$
3.	$8 \times \frac{3}{4}$	$9 \times \frac{5}{6}$	$4 \times \frac{4}{5}$
4.	$\frac{7}{8} \times 12$	$\frac{3}{5} \times 10$	$\frac{5}{6} \times 14$

Lesson 4   Problem Solving

Solve. Write each answer in simplest form.

1. A boy has a mass of 270 newtons (N) on Earth. His mass would be only $\frac{1}{6}$ of that on the moon. What would be his mass on the moon?

   His mass would be _____ N.

   1.

2. A woman has a mass of 530 N on Earth. What would be her mass on the moon?

   Her mass would be _____ N.

   2.

3. A dog has a mass of 90 N on Earth. Its mass would be only $\frac{2}{5}$ of that on Mars. What would be the dog's mass on Mars?

   It would have a mass of _____ N.

   3.

4. What would be the mass of the boy in problem 1 on Mars?

   His mass would be _____ N.

   4.

5. What would be the mass of the woman in problem 2 on Mars?

   Her mass would be _____ N.

   5.

6. A rock has a mass of 40 N on Earth. Its mass would be only $\frac{7}{8}$ of that on Venus. What would be the rock's mass on Venus?

   Its mass would be _____ N.

   6.

7. What would be the mass of the dog in problem 3 on Venus?

   Its mass would be _____ N.

   7.

Lesson 5 Multiplication (mixed numerals)

$2\frac{1}{6} \times 8 = \frac{13}{6} \times \frac{8}{1}$

Change the mixed numeral to a fraction. Name the whole number as a fraction.

$= \frac{13 \times 8}{6 \times 1}$

Multiply.

$= \frac{104}{6}$

$= 17\frac{1}{3}$

Change the answer to simplest form.

Write each answer in simplest form.

	a	*b*	*c*

1. $\quad 4\frac{1}{2} \times 5 \qquad\qquad 1\frac{3}{4} \times 7 \qquad\qquad 3 \times 2\frac{1}{8}$

2. $\quad 2\frac{2}{3} \times 6 \qquad\qquad 1\frac{7}{8} \times 6 \qquad\qquad 4 \times 2\frac{3}{8}$

3. $\quad 2\frac{4}{5} \times 7 \qquad\qquad 10 \times 2\frac{4}{15} \qquad\qquad 8\frac{1}{7} \times 4$

4. $\quad 8 \times 2\frac{5}{6} \qquad\qquad 3\frac{2}{7} \times 14 \qquad\qquad 3\frac{1}{3} \times 7$

Lesson 5 Problem Solving

Solve. Write each answer in simplest form.

1. It takes $3\frac{1}{2}$ tiles to make a pattern. How many tiles are needed to make seven patterns?

   _____ tiles are needed.

2. Suppose that 10 patterns like those in problem **1** were made. How many tiles would be needed?

   _____ tiles would be needed.

3. Julia can paint $1\frac{3}{4}$ walls in 1 h. How many walls can she paint in 5 h?

   She can paint _____ walls.

4. Each ceiling takes Julia $1\frac{5}{8}$ h to paint. How long would it take her to paint 6 ceilings?

   It would take her _____ h.

5. Suppose it takes $2\frac{5}{6}$ h to make an orbit around the moon. How long would it take to make 9 orbits?

   It would take _____ h.

6. There are 12 boxes of nails in each carton. There are $2\frac{1}{2}$ cartons. How many boxes of nails are there?

   There are _____ boxes of nails.

7. In problem **6,** suppose there are only six boxes in a carton. How many boxes of nails are there in $2\frac{1}{2}$ of these cartons?

   There are _____ boxes of nails.

8. It takes a model train $5\frac{3}{8}$ min to travel a loop of track. How long would it take the train to travel 10 loops of the track?

   It would take _____ min.

1.	
2.	
3.	
4.	
5.	
6.	
7.	
8.	

Lesson 6 Multiplication (mixed numerals)

$$1\frac{1}{2} \times 2\frac{1}{4} = \frac{3}{2} \times \frac{9}{4}$$

Change both mixed numerals to improper fractions.

$$= \frac{3 \times 9}{2 \times 4}$$

Multiply.

$$= \frac{27}{8}$$

$$= 3\frac{3}{8}$$

Change to simplest form.

Write each answer in simplest form.

	a	*b*	*c*
1.	$3\frac{1}{8} \times 1\frac{2}{3}$	$1\frac{1}{6} \times 2\frac{1}{2}$	$1\frac{4}{5} \times 1\frac{3}{4}$
2.	$2\frac{2}{3} \times 4\frac{1}{5}$	$2\frac{1}{2} \times 1\frac{1}{7}$	$1\frac{3}{5} \times 1\frac{1}{6}$
3.	$1\frac{3}{5} \times 3\frac{3}{4}$	$2\frac{1}{4} \times 3\frac{1}{3}$	$4\frac{1}{2} \times 2\frac{2}{3}$
4.	$2\frac{2}{5} \times 2\frac{1}{4}$	$1\frac{3}{8} \times 1\frac{3}{7}$	$2\frac{4}{5} \times 2\frac{6}{7}$

CHAPTER 11

Lesson 6　Problem Solving

Solve. Write each answer in simplest form.

1. Neptune completes $1\frac{1}{2}$ turns about its axis in 1 Earth day. How many turns does it complete in $2\frac{1}{2}$ Earth days?

    It completes _____ turns.

2. How many turns does Neptune complete in $5\frac{3}{4}$ Earth days?

    It completes _____ turns.

3. Mars takes $1\frac{9}{10}$ Earth years to orbit the Sun. How many Earth years does Mars take to orbit the Sun $3\frac{1}{2}$ times?

    It takes Mars _____ Earth years to orbit the Sun $3\frac{1}{2}$ times.

4. The distance between Toronto and Halifax is $2\frac{1}{2}$ times the distance from Toronto to Montreal. How many times the distance from Toronto to Montreal would you travel on $3\frac{1}{2}$ trips from Toronto to Halifax?

    You would travel _____ times the distance from Toronto to Montreal.

5. A boat can make the trip across the lake in $2\frac{1}{2}$ h. How long would it take to make $7\frac{1}{4}$ trips?

    It would take _____ h.

6. If it took the boat in problem 5 $3\frac{1}{4}$ h to cross the lake, how long would it take to make $7\frac{1}{4}$ trips?

    It would take _____ h.

7. How long would it take the boat in problem 5 to make 10 trips?

    It would take _____ h.

1.

2.

3.

4.

5.

6.

7.

Lesson 7   Multiplication Review

Write each answer in simplest form.

	a	b	c	d
1.	$\dfrac{3}{4} \times \dfrac{1}{5}$	$\dfrac{2}{7} \times \dfrac{3}{5}$	$\dfrac{2}{3} \times \dfrac{1}{5}$	$\dfrac{5}{12} \times \dfrac{7}{8}$
2.	$\dfrac{6}{7} \times \dfrac{1}{3}$	$\dfrac{4}{7} \times \dfrac{5}{6}$	$\dfrac{3}{8} \times \dfrac{2}{9}$	$\dfrac{3}{4} \times \dfrac{5}{12}$
3.	$6 \times \dfrac{2}{5}$	$\dfrac{2}{7} \times 4$	$8 \times \dfrac{3}{4}$	$\dfrac{3}{8} \times 6$
4.	$6\dfrac{2}{5} \times 5$	$6\dfrac{7}{8} \times 16$	$4 \times 5\dfrac{5}{6}$	$8 \times 2\dfrac{1}{12}$
5.	$3\dfrac{1}{8} \times 3\dfrac{1}{5}$	$4\dfrac{2}{3} \times 1\dfrac{4}{5}$	$2\dfrac{1}{2} \times 4\dfrac{2}{3}$	$1\dfrac{3}{5} \times 1\dfrac{1}{4}$

Lesson 7 Problem Solving

Solve. Write each answer in simplest form.

1. Zoe spent $\frac{2}{3}$ h doing homework. She spent $\frac{3}{4}$ of this time reading. How long did she spend reading?

   She spent _____ h reading.

2. A truck driver drives $8\frac{1}{2}$ h per day. How long will he drive in 10 days?

   He will drive _____ h.

3. In one hour a machine can produce $\frac{9}{10}$ of the silver required. Suppose the machine breaks down after $\frac{1}{3}$ h. How much of the silver required is processed?

   _____ of the silver required is processed.

4. Lola can type $\frac{3}{8}$ of a page per minute. How many pages can she type in 10 min?

   She can type _____ pages in 10 min.

5. There are 12 large boxes of Lotsa-clean detergent in a carton. There are $6\frac{3}{4}$ full cartons. How many boxes is this?

   There are _____ boxes.

6. There are $4\frac{1}{2}$ cartons of dog food. Each carton contains 3 bags? How many bags of dog food is this?

   There are _____ bags of dog food.

7. Chloe read 3 books in 2 weeks. Matt read $3\frac{1}{9}$ times as many books as Chloe. How many books did Matt read?

   Matt read _____ books.

1.
2.
3.
4.
5.
6.
7.

CHAPTER 11   PRACTICE TEST
Multiplication of Fractions

Write each answer in simplest form.

	a	*b*	*c*
1.	$\dfrac{7}{8} \times \dfrac{5}{6}$	$\dfrac{4}{5} \times \dfrac{3}{7}$	$\dfrac{2}{3} \times \dfrac{1}{5}$
2.	$\dfrac{2}{3} \times \dfrac{5}{6}$	$\dfrac{8}{9} \times \dfrac{3}{8}$	$\dfrac{2}{5} \times \dfrac{15}{16}$
3.	$8 \times \dfrac{3}{5}$	$9 \times \dfrac{5}{6}$	$\dfrac{3}{4} \times 20$
4.	$2\dfrac{2}{5} \times 4$	$4\dfrac{1}{4} \times 6$	$3 \times 1\dfrac{2}{9}$
5.	$\dfrac{2}{3} \times 1\dfrac{4}{5}$	$7\dfrac{1}{2} \times \dfrac{4}{5}$	$6\dfrac{1}{4} \times \dfrac{2}{5}$
6.	$1\dfrac{3}{5} \times 1\dfrac{1}{3}$	$2\dfrac{1}{2} \times 3\dfrac{1}{3}$	$2\dfrac{1}{6} \times 1\dfrac{1}{8}$

CHAPTER 12   PRETEST
Addition of Fractions

Write each answer in simplest form.

	a	*b*	*c*	*d*
1.	$\dfrac{1}{6}$ $+\dfrac{1}{6}$	$\dfrac{3}{8}$ $+\dfrac{1}{8}$	$\dfrac{5}{9}$ $+\dfrac{2}{9}$	$\dfrac{7}{12}$ $+\dfrac{5}{12}$
2.	$\dfrac{5}{6}$ $+\dfrac{1}{3}$	$\dfrac{7}{8}$ $+\dfrac{1}{2}$	$\dfrac{7}{10}$ $+\dfrac{2}{5}$	$\dfrac{3}{5}$ $+\dfrac{1}{4}$
3.	$7\dfrac{1}{2}$ $+3\dfrac{1}{4}$	$6\dfrac{7}{10}$ $+1\dfrac{1}{5}$	$5\dfrac{1}{3}$ $+\dfrac{3}{4}$	$4\dfrac{1}{3}$ $+2\dfrac{1}{2}$
4.	$1\dfrac{5}{8}$ $+4\dfrac{1}{6}$	$5\dfrac{3}{4}$ $+\dfrac{1}{5}$	$\dfrac{7}{12}$ $+\dfrac{5}{6}$	$\dfrac{1}{12}$ $+6\dfrac{3}{4}$
5.	$\dfrac{2}{3}$ $+\dfrac{3}{4}$	$9\dfrac{3}{8}$ $+\dfrac{1}{4}$	$3\dfrac{4}{5}$ $+1\dfrac{3}{10}$	$4\dfrac{2}{3}$ $+5\dfrac{5}{6}$

CHAPTER
12

Lesson 1   Addition (fractions)

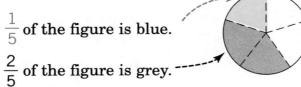

$\dfrac{1}{5}$ of the figure is blue.

$\dfrac{2}{5}$ of the figure is grey.

$\dfrac{3}{5}$ of the figure is coloured. $\dfrac{1}{5} + \dfrac{2}{5} = \dfrac{3}{5}$

Complete the following.

	a	*b*	*c*

1.

$\dfrac{1}{3} + \dfrac{1}{3} =$ $\dfrac{2}{4} + \dfrac{1}{4} =$ $\dfrac{1}{6} + \dfrac{4}{6} =$

2.

$\dfrac{2}{6} + \dfrac{3}{6} =$ $\dfrac{2}{7} + \dfrac{2}{7} =$ $\dfrac{5}{8} + \dfrac{2}{8} =$

3.

$\dfrac{1}{6} + \dfrac{0}{6} =$ $\dfrac{2}{9} + \dfrac{5}{9} =$ $\dfrac{2}{5} + \dfrac{1}{5} =$

4.

$\dfrac{3}{8} + \dfrac{2}{8} =$ $\dfrac{3}{5} + \dfrac{1}{5} =$ $\dfrac{4}{9} + \dfrac{4}{9} =$

CHAPTER 12

Lesson 2 Addition (like denominators)

Study how to add two fractions that have the same denominator.

Add the numerators.

$$\frac{3}{8} + \frac{2}{8} = \frac{3+2}{8} = \frac{5}{8}$$

Use the same denominator.

Add the numerators.

Use the same denominator.

___

Add.

	a	b	c	d	e
1.	$\frac{1}{3}$ $+\frac{1}{3}$	$\frac{2}{7}$ $+\frac{4}{7}$	$\frac{5}{8}$ $+\frac{2}{8}$	$\frac{1}{4}$ $+\frac{2}{4}$	$\frac{2}{5}$ $+\frac{2}{5}$
2.	$\frac{4}{9}$ $+\frac{3}{9}$	$\frac{4}{8}$ $+\frac{1}{8}$	$\frac{1}{6}$ $+\frac{4}{6}$	$\frac{3}{7}$ $+\frac{3}{7}$	$\frac{2}{10}$ $+\frac{5}{10}$
3.	$\frac{2}{5}$ $+\frac{1}{5}$	$\frac{3}{6}$ $+\frac{2}{6}$	$\frac{2}{8}$ $+\frac{1}{8}$	$\frac{2}{7}$ $+\frac{2}{7}$	$\frac{2}{9}$ $+\frac{2}{9}$
4.	$\frac{1}{9}$ $+\frac{4}{9}$	$\frac{1}{7}$ $+\frac{4}{7}$	$\frac{6}{8}$ $+\frac{1}{8}$	$\frac{1}{5}$ $+\frac{1}{5}$	$\frac{3}{7}$ $+\frac{1}{7}$

Lesson 3 Addition (like denominators)

$$\begin{array}{r}\dfrac{7}{10}\\[2mm]+\dfrac{9}{10}\\[1mm]\hline\end{array}$$

$$\dfrac{16}{10}=1\dfrac{3}{5}$$

Add.

Change to
simplest form.

$$\begin{array}{r}\dfrac{1}{12}\\[2mm]+\dfrac{11}{12}\\[1mm]\hline\end{array}$$

$$\dfrac{12}{12}=1$$

Add. Write each answer in simplest form.

	a	*b*	*c*	*d*
1.	$\dfrac{2}{3}$ $+\dfrac{2}{3}$	$\dfrac{4}{5}$ $+\dfrac{3}{5}$	$\dfrac{2}{9}$ $+\dfrac{1}{9}$	$\dfrac{1}{4}$ $+\dfrac{1}{4}$
2.	$\dfrac{1}{8}$ $+\dfrac{5}{8}$	$\dfrac{3}{10}$ $+\dfrac{9}{10}$	$\dfrac{3}{4}$ $+\dfrac{3}{4}$	$\dfrac{7}{12}$ $+\dfrac{11}{12}$
3.	$\dfrac{1}{2}$ $+\dfrac{1}{2}$	$\dfrac{6}{7}$ $+\dfrac{5}{7}$	$\dfrac{7}{8}$ $+\dfrac{7}{8}$	$\dfrac{5}{6}$ $+\dfrac{1}{6}$
4.	$\dfrac{3}{5}$ $+\dfrac{3}{5}$	$\dfrac{5}{12}$ $+\dfrac{7}{12}$	$\dfrac{8}{9}$ $+\dfrac{5}{9}$	$\dfrac{7}{10}$ $+\dfrac{9}{10}$

Lesson 4 Addition (mixed numerals)

$$4\frac{5}{8}$$

$$+2\frac{1}{8}$$

$$6\frac{6}{8} = 6\frac{3}{4}$$

Add the fractions.

Add the whole numbers.

Change to simplest form.

$$6\frac{7}{10}$$

$$+2\frac{9}{10}$$

$$8\frac{16}{10} = 9\frac{3}{5}$$

Add. Write each answer in simplest form.

	a	b	c	d

1. $1\frac{2}{5}$ $4\frac{1}{6}$ $3\frac{1}{10}$ $19\frac{3}{8}$

$\quad +2\frac{1}{5}$ $+2\frac{1}{6}$ $+2\frac{3}{10}$ $+7\frac{1}{8}$

2. $5\frac{3}{4}$ $6\frac{2}{3}$ $2\frac{9}{10}$ $26\frac{4}{5}$

$\quad +1\frac{3}{4}$ $+1\frac{1}{3}$ $+1\frac{7}{10}$ $+13\frac{3}{5}$

3. $4\frac{1}{2}$ $3\frac{5}{6}$ $8\frac{7}{12}$ $36\frac{7}{8}$

$\quad +2\frac{1}{2}$ $+4\frac{5}{6}$ $+4\frac{11}{12}$ $+27\frac{5}{8}$

4. $7\frac{2}{3}$ $9\frac{2}{5}$ $11\frac{3}{10}$ $58\frac{7}{9}$

$\quad +6\frac{2}{3}$ $+4\frac{4}{5}$ $+6\frac{7}{10}$ $+31\frac{5}{9}$

Lesson 5 Renaming Fractions

By separating the figure in different ways, you can write different fractions to tell how much is blue.

$\dfrac{2}{3}$ of the figure is blue. $\dfrac{4}{6}$ of the figure is blue.

$$\frac{2}{3} = \frac{4}{6}$$

$\dfrac{2}{3} = \dfrac{\blacksquare}{6}$ $\dfrac{2}{3} = \dfrac{\blacksquare}{9}$

$\dfrac{2}{3} = \dfrac{2 \times 2}{3 \times 2}$ **Multiply the numerator and the denominator by the same number.** $\dfrac{2}{3} = \dfrac{2 \times 3}{3 \times 3}$

$\dfrac{2}{3} = \dfrac{4}{6}$ $\dfrac{2}{3} = \dfrac{6}{9}$

Choose 2 so the new denominator is 6.   Choose 3 so the new denominator is 9.

Rename.

	a	*b*	*c*
1.	$\dfrac{2}{3} = \dfrac{\blacksquare}{12}$	$\dfrac{3}{4} = \dfrac{\blacksquare}{8}$	$\dfrac{5}{6} = \dfrac{\blacksquare}{12}$
2.	$\dfrac{1}{2} = \dfrac{\blacksquare}{10}$	$\dfrac{2}{5} = \dfrac{\blacksquare}{10}$	$\dfrac{3}{5} = \dfrac{\blacksquare}{15}$
3.	$\dfrac{3}{4} = \dfrac{\blacksquare}{12}$	$\dfrac{3}{8} = \dfrac{\blacksquare}{16}$	$\dfrac{4}{5} = \dfrac{\blacksquare}{20}$

CHAPTER 12

Lesson 5 Renaming Fractions

$$\frac{7}{8} = \frac{\blacksquare}{32}$$

$$\frac{7}{8} = \frac{7 \times 4}{8 \times 4}$$

$$\frac{7}{8} = \frac{28}{32}$$

$$7 = \frac{\blacksquare}{3}$$

$$\frac{7}{1} = \frac{7 \times 3}{1 \times 3}$$

$$7 = \frac{21}{3}$$

Name the whole number as a fraction whose denominator is 1. Then rename.

Rename.

	a	*b*	*c*
1.	$\frac{1}{2} = \frac{\blacksquare}{4}$	$\frac{1}{3} = \frac{\blacksquare}{9}$	$3 = \frac{\blacksquare}{12}$
2.	$6 = \frac{\blacksquare}{2}$	$\frac{4}{5} = \frac{\blacksquare}{10}$	$7 = \frac{\blacksquare}{5}$
3.	$\frac{1}{4} = \frac{\blacksquare}{8}$	$\frac{2}{3} = \frac{\blacksquare}{15}$	$4 = \frac{\blacksquare}{3}$
4.	$\frac{1}{3} = \frac{\blacksquare}{6}$	$\frac{1}{2} = \frac{\blacksquare}{8}$	$6 = \frac{\blacksquare}{6}$

Lesson 6 Addition (unlike denominators)

> When adding fractions that have different denominators, rename the fractions so they have the same denominator.

$$\begin{array}{r}\dfrac{1}{3} \\[4pt] +\dfrac{1}{2}\end{array} \quad \begin{array}{c}\times\dfrac{2}{2} \\[4pt] \times\dfrac{3}{3}\end{array} \quad \begin{array}{r}\dfrac{2}{6} \\[4pt] +\dfrac{3}{6} \\ \hline \dfrac{5}{6}\end{array}$$

The denominators are 2 and 3. Since $2 \times 3 = 6$, rename each fraction with a denominator of 6.

Then add the fractions.

$$\begin{array}{r}\dfrac{1}{2} \\[4pt] +\dfrac{2}{3}\end{array} \quad \begin{array}{c}\times\dfrac{3}{3} \\[4pt] \times\dfrac{2}{2}\end{array} \quad \begin{array}{r}\dfrac{3}{6} \\[4pt] +\dfrac{4}{6} \\ \hline \end{array}$$

$$\dfrac{7}{6} = 1\dfrac{1}{6}$$

Change $\frac{7}{6}$ to a mixed numeral in simplest form.

Write each answer in simplest form.

	a	*b*	*c*	*d*
1.	$\dfrac{2}{5}$ $+\dfrac{1}{2}$	$\dfrac{1}{4}$ $+\dfrac{2}{3}$	$\dfrac{2}{5}$ $+\dfrac{1}{3}$	$\dfrac{1}{2}$ $+\dfrac{1}{5}$
2.	$\dfrac{5}{6}$ $+\dfrac{3}{5}$	$\dfrac{2}{3}$ $+\dfrac{1}{5}$	$\dfrac{1}{3}$ $+\dfrac{3}{10}$	$\dfrac{5}{8}$ $+\dfrac{2}{3}$
3.	$\dfrac{3}{4}$ $+\dfrac{1}{3}$	$\dfrac{2}{3}$ $+\dfrac{4}{5}$	$\dfrac{2}{3}$ $+\dfrac{3}{4}$	$\dfrac{7}{8}$ $+\dfrac{1}{3}$

Lesson 6 Addition

$$\frac{2}{5} \quad \times\frac{2}{2} \quad \frac{4}{10}$$
$$+\frac{3}{10} \longrightarrow +\frac{3}{10}$$
$$\frac{7}{10}$$

The denominators are 5 and 10. Since $2 \times 5 = 10$, rename only $\frac{2}{5}$ with a denominator of 10.

Then add the fractions.

$$\frac{7}{10} \longrightarrow \frac{7}{10}$$
$$+\frac{2}{5} \quad \times\frac{2}{2} \quad +\frac{4}{10}$$
$$\frac{11}{10} = 1\frac{1}{10} \quad \text{Change } \tfrac{11}{10} \text{ to simplest form.}$$

Write each answer in simplest form.

	a	b	c	d

1.
$$\frac{3}{4} \qquad \frac{2}{3} \qquad \frac{1}{2} \qquad \frac{5}{12}$$
$$+\frac{1}{8} \qquad +\frac{5}{6} \qquad +\frac{3}{10} \qquad +\frac{2}{3}$$

2.
$$\frac{5}{16} \qquad \frac{1}{6} \qquad \frac{5}{8} \qquad \frac{9}{10}$$
$$+\frac{3}{8} \qquad +\frac{1}{2} \qquad +\frac{1}{4} \qquad +\frac{3}{5}$$

3.
$$\frac{3}{4} \qquad \frac{5}{12} \qquad \frac{5}{6} \qquad \frac{1}{2}$$
$$+\frac{9}{16} \qquad +\frac{1}{4} \qquad +\frac{1}{3} \qquad +\frac{7}{8}$$

Lesson 7 Addition (unlike denominators)

$$\frac{1}{6} \times \frac{4}{4} \quad \frac{4}{24}$$

$$+\frac{5}{8} \times \frac{3}{3} \quad +\frac{15}{24}$$

$$\frac{19}{24}$$

The denominators are 6 and 8. Since $4 \times 6 = 24$ and $3 \times 8 = 24$, rename each fraction with a denominator of 24.

Then add the fractions.

$$\frac{5}{6} \times \frac{4}{4} \quad \frac{20}{24}$$

$$+\frac{3}{8} \times \frac{3}{3} \quad +\frac{9}{24}$$

$$\frac{29}{24} = 1\frac{5}{24}$$

Change $\frac{29}{24}$ to simplest form.

Write each answer in simplest form.

	a	b	c	d
1.	$\frac{1}{9}$ $+\frac{1}{6}$	$\frac{1}{6}$ $+\frac{1}{4}$	$\frac{5}{6}$ $+\frac{1}{8}$	$\frac{1}{10}$ $+\frac{1}{12}$
2.	$\frac{1}{6}$ $+\frac{3}{8}$	$\frac{3}{4}$ $+\frac{1}{6}$	$\frac{5}{6}$ $+\frac{5}{8}$	$\frac{3}{10}$ $+\frac{3}{8}$
3.	$\frac{3}{10}$ $+\frac{5}{12}$	$\frac{5}{6}$ $+\frac{4}{9}$	$\frac{3}{10}$ $+\frac{1}{4}$	$\frac{5}{6}$ $+\frac{3}{10}$
4.	$\frac{7}{10}$ $+\frac{5}{6}$	$\frac{11}{12}$ $+\frac{7}{8}$	$\frac{9}{10}$ $+\frac{7}{8}$	$\frac{1}{4}$ $+\frac{5}{6}$

CHAPTER 12

Lesson 7 Problem Solving

Solve. Write each answer in simplest form.

1. To make green paint, Andrea mixed $\frac{7}{8}$ can of yellow paint and $\frac{1}{2}$ can of blue paint. How much green paint did she make?

   She made _____ cans of green paint.

2. Sean painted $\frac{1}{3}$ of a fence. Sandra painted $\frac{1}{4}$ of the fence. How much of the fence did they paint?

   They painted _____ of the fence.

3. Maureen bought $\frac{3}{4}$ of a round of cheese. Chang bought $\frac{1}{2}$ of a round of cheese. How much cheese did they buy?

   They bought _____ rounds of cheese.

4. Joy used $\frac{2}{3}$ of a bag of milk in three bowls of cereal, and then $\frac{3}{4}$ of a bag to make milkshakes. How many bags of milk did Joy use?

   Joy used _____ bags of milk.

5. Elisabeth read $\frac{1}{2}$ of a book on Monday, and $\frac{3}{8}$ of the book on Tuesday. How much of the book did she read on the 2 days?

   She read _____ of the book.

6. Richard used $\frac{3}{4}$ of a can of paint on Saturday. He used $\frac{13}{16}$ of a can of paint on Sunday. How much paint did he use altogether?

   He used _____ cans of paint.

7. It rained for $\frac{3}{10}$ h yesterday and $\frac{3}{4}$ h today. How long did it rain on the 2 days?

   It rained for _____ h on the 2 days.

1.	
2.	**3.**
4.	**5.**
6.	**7.**

Lesson 8 Addition (mixed numerals)

Rename the fractions so they have the same denominator.

$3\frac{1}{4} \longrightarrow 3\frac{3}{12}$

$+2\frac{5}{6} \longrightarrow +2\frac{10}{12}$

$5\frac{13}{12} = 6\frac{1}{12}$ Change to simplest form.

$4\frac{1}{2} \longrightarrow 4\frac{3}{6}$

$+3\frac{2}{3} \longrightarrow +3\frac{4}{6}$

$7\frac{7}{6} = 8\frac{1}{6}$

Write each answer in simplest form.

	a	b	c	d

1. $3\frac{5}{6}$ $+4\frac{5}{8}$ $5\frac{2}{3}$ $+1\frac{5}{6}$ $6\frac{5}{6}$ $+3\frac{1}{4}$ $\frac{1}{2}$ $+2\frac{3}{4}$

2. $1\frac{5}{6}$ $+4\frac{1}{3}$ $5\frac{1}{2}$ $+2\frac{3}{4}$ $3\frac{2}{3}$ $+\frac{3}{4}$ $2\frac{3}{5}$ $+1\frac{1}{2}$

3. $4\frac{3}{8}$ $+6\frac{1}{4}$ $5\frac{1}{3}$ $+\frac{2}{5}$ $4\frac{2}{5}$ $+2\frac{3}{10}$ $2\frac{1}{8}$ $+5\frac{3}{4}$

4. $3\frac{1}{2}$ $+3\frac{1}{2}$ $1\frac{3}{8}$ $+2\frac{1}{2}$ $9\frac{3}{4}$ $+6\frac{1}{2}$ $12\frac{2}{3}$ $+1\frac{5}{6}$

CHAPTER 12

Lesson 8 Problem Solving

Solve each problem.

1. Jennifer spent $1\frac{1}{2}$ h working on Ms. Thomkin's car on Monday. She spent $2\frac{3}{4}$ h more on Tuesday to finish the tune-up. How many hours in all did she work on Ms. Thomkin's car?

   She worked _____ h in all.

   1.

2. Marissa worked $7\frac{1}{4}$ h on Monday. She worked $9\frac{3}{4}$ h on Tuesday. How many hours did she work in all on Monday and Tuesday?

   She worked _____ h in all on Monday and Tuesday.

   2.

3. The auto repair shop is $1\frac{3}{10}$ km from the bank. The bank is $3\frac{3}{5}$ km from Gina's home. After she left her car at the shop, Gina walked to the bank. Then she walked home. How far did Gina walk in all?

   Gina walked _____ km.

   3.

4. It took $2\frac{5}{6}$ h to fix Mrs. Sax's car. It took $3\frac{1}{2}$ h to fix Mr. Wong's car. How long did it take to fix both cars?

   It took _____ h to fix both cars.

   4.

Lesson 9 Addition Review

Write each answer in simplest form.

	a	*b*	*c*	*d*
1.	$\dfrac{1}{12}$ $+\dfrac{1}{6}$	$5\dfrac{5}{6}$ $+3\dfrac{5}{8}$	$4\dfrac{1}{3}$ $+2\dfrac{3}{4}$	$\dfrac{9}{16}$ $+\dfrac{3}{4}$
2.	$1\dfrac{1}{4}$ $+6\dfrac{3}{5}$	$\dfrac{4}{7}$ $+\dfrac{9}{10}$	$3\dfrac{3}{4}$ $+\dfrac{9}{10}$	$\dfrac{7}{18}$ $+\dfrac{7}{9}$
3.	$\dfrac{5}{7}$ $+\dfrac{1}{2}$	$4\dfrac{2}{5}$ $+2\dfrac{8}{15}$	$\dfrac{5}{12}$ $+5\dfrac{3}{4}$	$\dfrac{9}{14}$ $+\dfrac{3}{4}$
4.	$2\dfrac{1}{10}$ $+1\dfrac{1}{6}$	$\dfrac{1}{12}$ $+\dfrac{5}{9}$	$\dfrac{5}{6}$ $+\dfrac{1}{2}$	$8\dfrac{1}{3}$ $+3\dfrac{2}{9}$
5.	$\dfrac{2}{5}$ $+\dfrac{3}{10}$	$\dfrac{7}{9}$ $+1\dfrac{1}{6}$	$5\dfrac{2}{5}$ $+3\dfrac{7}{10}$	$7\dfrac{3}{4}$ $+9\dfrac{5}{6}$

Lesson 9 Problem Solving

Solve. Write each answer in simplest form.

1. Emilio planted $3\frac{1}{2}$ rows of corn and $2\frac{3}{4}$ rows of beans. How many rows did he plant altogether?

   He planted _____ rows.

2. Arlene spent $2\frac{1}{2}$ h planting part of a garden. It took her $1\frac{3}{4}$ h to finish planting the garden. How long did it take to plant the garden?

   It took _____ h.

3. It takes April $\frac{3}{4}$ h to fall asleep, and then she sleeps for $8\frac{1}{2}$ h. How long is April in bed?

   April is in bed for _____ h.

4. June's school is $6\frac{1}{2}$ blocks from her house. The grocery store is $7\frac{3}{4}$ blocks from the school. How far is it from June's house to the grocery store?

   It is _____ blocks.

5. Ned can run 10 km in $1\frac{1}{8}$ h. Phil can run 10 km in $\frac{1}{10}$ of an hour longer. How long does it take phil to run 10 km?

   It takes Phil _____ h to run 10 km.

6. Jake used $1\frac{7}{12}$ cartons of eggs last week and $2\frac{5}{12}$ cartons this week. How many cartons of eggs did he use in the 2 weeks?

   He used _____ cartons of eggs.

1.	2.
3.	4.
5.	6.

Lesson 10 Addition Review

Write each answer in simplest form.

	a	*b*	*c*	*d*

1. $\frac{1}{9}$ $+\frac{4}{9}$ $\frac{2}{7}$ $+\frac{3}{7}$ $\frac{8}{9}$ $+\frac{5}{9}$ $\frac{11}{16}$ $+\frac{7}{16}$

2. $\frac{2}{3}$ $+\frac{1}{5}$ $\frac{2}{5}$ $+\frac{3}{4}$ $\frac{1}{2}$ $+\frac{3}{4}$ $\frac{5}{6}$ $+\frac{1}{12}$

3. $\frac{7}{8}$ $+\frac{5}{6}$ $\frac{5}{12}$ $+\frac{1}{3}$ $\frac{1}{5}$ $+\frac{7}{10}$ $\frac{7}{8}$ $+\frac{5}{12}$

4. $\frac{2}{5}$ $+\frac{1}{5}$ $2\frac{1}{9}$ $+\frac{1}{3}$ $7\frac{5}{8}$ $+\frac{2}{3}$ $4\frac{7}{12}$ $+1\frac{1}{2}$

5. $\frac{1}{5}$ $+\frac{1}{3}$ $\frac{3}{4}$ $+\frac{1}{5}$ $1\frac{2}{3}$ $+1\frac{5}{6}$ $3\frac{11}{12}$ $+2\frac{5}{6}$

Lesson 10 Problem Solving

Solve. Write each answer in simplest form.

1. Jared lives $\frac{7}{8}$ of a block from the stadium and $\frac{3}{8}$ of a block from the school. He walked home from school and then to the stadium. How far did he walk?

   Jared walked _____ blocks.

2. Courtney read for $\frac{5}{6}$ h before dinner. After dinner she read for $\frac{2}{5}$ h. How long did she read?

   Courtney read _____ h in all.

3. The Clements family drank $\frac{3}{4}$ of a carton of milk for dinner. There was $\frac{1}{8}$ of a carton left. How much milk was there before dinner?

   There was _____ of a carton of milk.

4. Gary sprinted $1\frac{3}{10}$ laps around the track. Glen sprinted $\frac{3}{10}$ of a lap more. How far did Glen sprint?

   Glen sprinted _____ laps.

5. Rocio read $4\frac{3}{4}$ books last week. His sister read $1\frac{1}{2}$ more books. How many books did Rocio's sister read?

   Rocio's sister read _____ books.

6. To make pale blue paint, Lynn mixed $2\frac{1}{2}$ cans of blue paint and $3\frac{3}{4}$ cans of white paint. How much pale blue paint did she make?

   She made _____ cans of pale blue paint.

7. Last year Becky could run for $49\frac{1}{2}$ min without stopping. Since then she has added $1\frac{7}{8}$ min. How long can she run now?

   She can now run for _____ min.

1.	
2.	**3.**
4.	**5.**
6.	**7.**

CHAPTER 12   PRACTICE TEST
Addition of Fractions

Write each answer in simplest form.

	a	*b*	*c*	*d*

1.

$$\begin{array}{r} \frac{3}{10} \\ +\frac{1}{10} \\ \hline \end{array}$$
$$\begin{array}{r} \frac{5}{6} \\ +\frac{1}{6} \\ \hline \end{array}$$
$$\begin{array}{r} \frac{7}{8} \\ +\frac{5}{8} \\ \hline \end{array}$$
$$\begin{array}{r} \frac{4}{7} \\ +\frac{1}{7} \\ \hline \end{array}$$

2.

$$\begin{array}{r} \frac{5}{8} \\ +\frac{1}{4} \\ \hline \end{array}$$
$$\begin{array}{r} \frac{3}{10} \\ +\frac{3}{4} \\ \hline \end{array}$$
$$\begin{array}{r} \frac{1}{2} \\ +\frac{4}{5} \\ \hline \end{array}$$
$$\begin{array}{r} \frac{5}{6} \\ +\frac{3}{4} \\ \hline \end{array}$$

3.

$$\begin{array}{r} 5\frac{3}{10} \\ +1\frac{1}{3} \\ \hline \end{array}$$
$$\begin{array}{r} 4\frac{2}{9} \\ +2\frac{2}{3} \\ \hline \end{array}$$
$$\begin{array}{r} \frac{5}{6} \\ +3\frac{1}{12} \\ \hline \end{array}$$
$$\begin{array}{r} 6\frac{5}{12} \\ +\frac{1}{3} \\ \hline \end{array}$$

4.

$$\begin{array}{r} 1\frac{3}{4} \\ +4\frac{7}{10} \\ \hline \end{array}$$
$$\begin{array}{r} 5\frac{1}{3} \\ +\frac{4}{5} \\ \hline \end{array}$$
$$\begin{array}{r} 2\frac{3}{4} \\ +6\frac{15}{16} \\ \hline \end{array}$$
$$\begin{array}{r} 7\frac{7}{10} \\ +8\frac{4}{5} \\ \hline \end{array}$$

5.

$$\begin{array}{r} 7\frac{1}{5} \\ +\frac{1}{4} \\ \hline \end{array}$$
$$\begin{array}{r} 9\frac{9}{10} \\ +\frac{7}{12} \\ \hline \end{array}$$
$$\begin{array}{r} 42\frac{5}{6} \\ +5\frac{2}{3} \\ \hline \end{array}$$
$$\begin{array}{r} 54\frac{1}{2} \\ +21\frac{4}{5} \\ \hline \end{array}$$

CHAPTER 13   PRETEST
Subtraction of Fractions

Write each answer in simplest form.

	a	b	c	d

1.
$$\frac{7}{8}$$
$$-\frac{3}{8}$$

$$\frac{8}{9}$$
$$-\frac{2}{9}$$

$$\frac{5}{6}$$
$$-\frac{1}{6}$$

$$\frac{11}{12}$$
$$-\frac{3}{12}$$

2.
$$5\frac{4}{5}$$
$$-2\frac{1}{5}$$

$$4\frac{5}{9}$$
$$-3\frac{2}{9}$$

$$6\frac{4}{7}$$
$$-1\frac{6}{7}$$

$$3\frac{3}{8}$$
$$-\frac{7}{8}$$

3.
$$\frac{5}{6}$$
$$-\frac{2}{3}$$

$$\frac{2}{3}$$
$$-\frac{1}{2}$$

$$\frac{8}{9}$$
$$-\frac{1}{3}$$

$$\frac{7}{8}$$
$$-\frac{3}{4}$$

4.
$$\frac{7}{10}$$
$$-\frac{1}{5}$$

$$\frac{7}{8}$$
$$-\frac{3}{10}$$

$$\frac{9}{10}$$
$$-\frac{2}{5}$$

$$\frac{5}{6}$$
$$-\frac{7}{12}$$

5.
$$4\frac{5}{6}$$
$$-2\frac{1}{3}$$

$$3\frac{7}{8}$$
$$-1\frac{2}{3}$$

$$2\frac{1}{10}$$
$$-1\frac{4}{5}$$

$$2\frac{1}{5}$$
$$-\frac{2}{3}$$

CHAPTER 13

Lesson 1 Subtraction (like denominators)

Study how to subtract when fractions have the same denominator.

Subtract the numerators.

$$\frac{7}{8} - \frac{5}{8} = \frac{7-5}{8} = \frac{2}{8} = \frac{1}{4}$$

Use the same denominator.   Change to simplest form.

Subtract the numerators.

$$\begin{array}{r} \frac{7}{8} \\ -\frac{5}{8} \\ \hline \frac{2}{8} = \frac{1}{4} \end{array}$$

Use the same denominator.

Change to simplest form.

Write each answer in simplest form.

	a	*b*	*c*	*d*	*e*
1.	$\begin{array}{r}\frac{5}{9}\\-\frac{4}{9}\\\hline\end{array}$	$\begin{array}{r}\frac{3}{5}\\-\frac{1}{5}\\\hline\end{array}$	$\begin{array}{r}\frac{8}{9}\\-\frac{4}{9}\\\hline\end{array}$	$\begin{array}{r}\frac{3}{4}\\-\frac{1}{4}\\\hline\end{array}$	$\begin{array}{r}\frac{5}{6}\\-\frac{1}{6}\\\hline\end{array}$
2.	$\begin{array}{r}\frac{6}{7}\\-\frac{4}{7}\\\hline\end{array}$	$\begin{array}{r}\frac{5}{8}\\-\frac{3}{8}\\\hline\end{array}$	$\begin{array}{r}\frac{9}{10}\\-\frac{3}{10}\\\hline\end{array}$	$\begin{array}{r}\frac{2}{5}\\-\frac{1}{5}\\\hline\end{array}$	$\begin{array}{r}\frac{5}{9}\\-\frac{1}{9}\\\hline\end{array}$
3.	$\begin{array}{r}\frac{5}{7}\\-\frac{2}{7}\\\hline\end{array}$	$\begin{array}{r}\frac{8}{9}\\-\frac{1}{9}\\\hline\end{array}$	$\begin{array}{r}\frac{7}{8}\\-\frac{3}{8}\\\hline\end{array}$	$\begin{array}{r}\frac{7}{12}\\-\frac{5}{12}\\\hline\end{array}$	$\begin{array}{r}\frac{9}{10}\\-\frac{7}{10}\\\hline\end{array}$
4.	$\begin{array}{r}\frac{4}{5}\\-\frac{2}{5}\\\hline\end{array}$	$\begin{array}{r}\frac{2}{3}\\-\frac{1}{3}\\\hline\end{array}$	$\begin{array}{r}\frac{7}{10}\\-\frac{3}{10}\\\hline\end{array}$	$\begin{array}{r}\frac{7}{9}\\-\frac{4}{9}\\\hline\end{array}$	$\begin{array}{r}\frac{7}{8}\\-\frac{1}{8}\\\hline\end{array}$

CHAPTER 13

Lesson 2 Subtraction (from whole numbers)

Rename the whole number as a mixed numeral so
the denominator is the same as that of the fraction.

$$2 \longrightarrow 1\frac{4}{4}$$

$$\begin{array}{c} 2 = 1 + 1 \\ = 1 + \frac{4}{4} \\ = 1\frac{4}{4} \end{array}$$

$$-\frac{3}{4} \longrightarrow -\frac{3}{4}$$

$$1\frac{1}{4}$$

$$5 \longrightarrow 4\frac{8}{8}$$

$$\begin{array}{c} 5 = 4 + 1 \\ = 4 + \frac{8}{8} \\ = 4\frac{8}{8} \end{array}$$

$$-\frac{7}{8} \longrightarrow -\frac{7}{8}$$

$$4\frac{1}{8}$$

Write each answer in simplest form.

	a	b	c	d
1.	2 $-\frac{1}{4}$	3 $-\frac{2}{3}$	6 $-\frac{1}{5}$	5 $-\frac{1}{3}$
2.	4 $-\frac{3}{4}$	5 $-\frac{2}{5}$	4 $-\frac{2}{5}$	6 $-\frac{5}{6}$
3.	1 $-\frac{1}{2}$	2 $-\frac{7}{8}$	1 $-\frac{1}{8}$	2 $-\frac{3}{10}$

Lesson 3 Subtraction (mixed numerals)

$\frac{1}{4}$ is less than $\frac{3}{4}$. So rename $7\frac{1}{4}$ as shown so you can subtract the fractions.

$$7\frac{1}{4} \longrightarrow 6\frac{5}{4}$$
$$-1\frac{3}{4} \longrightarrow -1\frac{3}{4}$$
$$\overline{5\frac{2}{4}} = 5\frac{1}{2}$$

$7\frac{1}{4} = 6 + 1 + \frac{1}{4}$
$= 6 + \frac{4}{4} + \frac{1}{4}$
$= 6\frac{5}{4}$

Change to simplest form.

$\frac{1}{3}$ is less than $\frac{2}{3}$. So rename $3\frac{1}{3}$ as shown so you can subtract the fractions.

$$3\frac{1}{3} \longrightarrow 2\frac{4}{3}$$
$$-2\frac{2}{3} \longrightarrow -2\frac{2}{3}$$
$$\overline{\frac{2}{3}}$$

$3\frac{1}{3} = 2 + 1 + \frac{1}{3}$
$= 2 + \frac{3}{3} + \frac{1}{3}$
$= 2\frac{4}{3}$

Write each answer in simplest form.

	a	b	c	d
1.	$5\frac{8}{9}$ $-2\frac{6}{9}$	$4\frac{6}{7}$ $-2\frac{1}{7}$	$8\frac{9}{10}$ $-3\frac{4}{10}$	$6\frac{3}{8}$ $-2\frac{1}{8}$
2.	$5\frac{1}{3}$ $-1\frac{2}{3}$	$7\frac{2}{5}$ $-1\frac{4}{5}$	$8\frac{3}{8}$ $-2\frac{5}{8}$	$6\frac{1}{9}$ $-2\frac{6}{9}$
3.	$5\frac{3}{12}$ $-2\frac{11}{12}$	$4\frac{5}{6}$ $-2\frac{2}{6}$	$3\frac{2}{5}$ $-1\frac{4}{5}$	$7\frac{2}{3}$ $-6\frac{2}{3}$

CHAPTER 13

Lesson 3 Problem Solving

Solve. Write each answer in simplest form.

1. Hank's workday is 9 h long. His lunch and breaks total $1\frac{1}{2}$ h. How many hours is Hank actually working per day?

    Hank is actually working _____ h per day.

2. Sue says it will take $6\frac{1}{6}$ h to travel to her grandparents' home. She has been travelling $3\frac{5}{6}$ h. How much longer will it be before she gets there?

    It will be _____ h longer.

3. Don ran 5 laps yesterday and $3\frac{1}{2}$ laps today. How many more laps did Don run yesterday than today?

    Don ran _____ laps more yesterday.

4. FloTime stock was $\$29\frac{1}{2}$ yesterday and $\$27$ today. By how much did the stock price go down?

    The stock price went down $ _____.

5. This year Reola spends $5\frac{1}{4}$ h in school each day. Last year she spent $4\frac{3}{4}$ h in school each day. How many more hours does she spend in school each day this year than last year?

    She spends _____ h more in school each day this year than last year.

6. A wire is $4\frac{7}{12}$ m long. Suppose $\frac{11}{12}$ m of wire is used. How much wire would be left?

    _____ m of wire would be left.

1.	2.
3.	4.
5.	6.

Lesson 4 Subtraction (unlike denominators)

When subtracting fractions that have different denominators, rename the fractions so they have the same denominator.

$$\frac{2}{3} \times \frac{4}{4} = \frac{8}{12}$$
$$-\frac{1}{4} \times \frac{3}{3} = -\frac{3}{12}$$
$$\frac{5}{12}$$

Since $3 \times 4 = 12$, rename each fraction with a denominator of 12. Then subtract.

$$\frac{5}{6} \longrightarrow \frac{5}{6}$$
$$-\frac{1}{2} \times \frac{3}{3} = -\frac{3}{6}$$
$$\frac{2}{6} = \frac{1}{3}$$

Since $2 \times 3 = 6$, rename only $\frac{1}{2}$ with a denominator of 6. Then subtract.

Write each answer in simplest form.

	a	b	c	d
1.	$\frac{3}{5}$ $-\frac{1}{3}$	$\frac{5}{6}$ $-\frac{2}{5}$	$\frac{7}{8}$ $-\frac{1}{2}$	$\frac{2}{3}$ $-\frac{4}{9}$
2.	$\frac{5}{6}$ $-\frac{1}{3}$	$\frac{2}{3}$ $-\frac{1}{6}$	$\frac{7}{12}$ $-\frac{1}{4}$	$\frac{4}{5}$ $-\frac{3}{10}$
3.	$\frac{9}{10}$ $-\frac{1}{2}$	$\frac{5}{6}$ $-\frac{3}{7}$	$\frac{3}{4}$ $-\frac{1}{5}$	$\frac{11}{12}$ $-\frac{1}{6}$

CHAPTER 13

Lesson 4 Problem Solving

Solve. Write each answer in simplest form.

1. Phillip jogged $\frac{5}{6}$ of a block. He walked $\frac{1}{2}$ of a block. How much farther did he jog than he walked?

   1. _____

   He jogged _____ of a block farther than he walked.

2. Kyle and Eric have painted $\frac{2}{3}$ of a room. Kyle painted $\frac{1}{2}$ of the room. How much of the room did Eric paint?

   2. _____

   Eric painted _____ of the room.

3. Rona and Joan have $\frac{5}{6}$ of a room painted. Joan painted $\frac{1}{5}$ of the room. How much of the room did Rona paint?

   3. _____

   Rona painted _____ of the room.

4. Ardith had $\frac{3}{4}$ of a carton of eggs. She used $\frac{7}{12}$ of a carton for breakfast. How much of a carton does she have left?

   4. _____

   She has _____ of a carton of eggs left.

5. Barb ran $\frac{9}{16}$ of a lap of the track. Jim ran $\frac{1}{4}$ of a lap of the track. How much more of a lap did Barb run than Jim?

   5. _____

   Barb ran _____ of a lap more than Jim.

6. It takes Monica $\frac{5}{6}$ h to get to work. In doing so, she rides the train $\frac{2}{3}$ h. She walks the remaining time. How much time does she spend walking to work?

   6. _____

   She spends _____ h walking to work.

7. Mr. Anthony and Mr. Androtti completed $\frac{3}{4}$ of a job. Mr. Androtti completed $\frac{2}{9}$ of the job. What part of the job did Mr. Anthony complete?

   7. _____

   Mr. Anthony completed _____ of the job.

Lesson 5 Subtraction (unlike denominators)

$$\frac{3}{4} \longrightarrow \frac{15}{20}$$
$$\frac{-\frac{3}{5}}{} \longrightarrow \frac{-\frac{12}{20}}{\frac{3}{20}}$$

$$\frac{9}{10} \longrightarrow \frac{27}{30}$$
$$\frac{-\frac{11}{15}}{} \longrightarrow \frac{-\frac{22}{30}}{\frac{5}{30} = \frac{1}{6}}$$

Write each answer in simplest form.

	a	b	c	d
1.	$\frac{5}{6}$ $-\frac{3}{8}$	$\frac{3}{4}$ $-\frac{1}{6}$	$\frac{7}{8}$ $-\frac{3}{10}$	$\frac{5}{6}$ $-\frac{2}{9}$
2.	$\frac{9}{10}$ $-\frac{3}{5}$	$\frac{7}{8}$ $-\frac{1}{6}$	$\frac{2}{3}$ $-\frac{1}{5}$	$\frac{8}{9}$ $-\frac{5}{6}$
3.	$\frac{3}{4}$ $-\frac{5}{12}$	$\frac{7}{12}$ $-\frac{1}{4}$	$\frac{7}{8}$ $-\frac{1}{3}$	$\frac{3}{10}$ $-\frac{1}{4}$
4.	$\frac{2}{3}$ $-\frac{4}{9}$	$\frac{11}{12}$ $-\frac{3}{8}$	$\frac{1}{4}$ $-\frac{1}{12}$	$\frac{2}{3}$ $-\frac{7}{12}$

CHAPTER 13

Lesson 5 Problem Solving

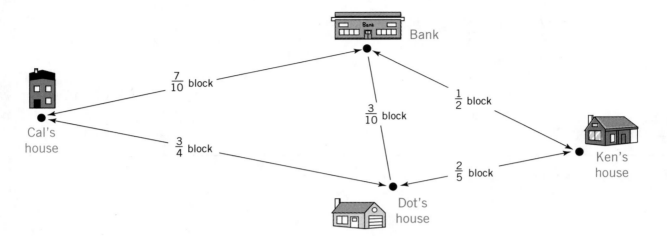

Solve. Write each answer in simplest form.

1. Who lives farther from the bank, Cal or Dot? How much farther?

_____ lives _____ of a block farther.

2. Who lives farther from the bank, Ken or Cal? How much farther?

_____ lives _____ of a block farther.

3. How much farther is it from Dot's house to Cal's house than from Dot's house to the bank?

It is _____ of a block farther.

4. How much farther is it from Dot's house to Ken's house than from Dot's house to the bank?

It is _____ of a block farther.

5. Cal walked from his house to Dot's house. Ken walked from his house to Dot's house. Who walked farther? How much farther?

_____ walked _____ of a block farther.

1.

2.

3.

4.

5.

Lesson 6 Subtraction (mixed numerals)

Rename so the fractions have the same denominator.

Rename $7\frac{3}{12}$ so you can subtract.

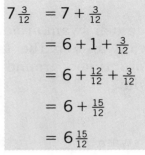

$$7\frac{3}{12} = 7 + \frac{3}{12}$$
$$= 6 + 1 + \frac{3}{12}$$
$$= 6 + \frac{12}{12} + \frac{3}{12}$$
$$= 6 + \frac{15}{12}$$
$$= 6\frac{15}{12}$$

$$7\frac{1}{4} \longrightarrow 7\frac{3}{12} \longrightarrow 6\frac{15}{12}$$
$$-3\frac{2}{3} \longrightarrow -3\frac{8}{12} \longrightarrow -3\frac{8}{12}$$
$$3\frac{7}{12}$$

Write each answer in simplest form.

	a	b	c	d
1.	$5\frac{1}{3}$ $-3\frac{3}{4}$	$7\frac{3}{5}$ $-4\frac{7}{10}$	$6\frac{1}{6}$ $-1\frac{3}{8}$	$5\frac{4}{9}$ $-2\frac{1}{3}$
2.	$4\frac{3}{8}$ $-2\frac{1}{3}$	$3\frac{5}{6}$ $-2\frac{1}{12}$	$6\frac{4}{7}$ $-5\frac{1}{2}$	$6\frac{3}{5}$ $-2\frac{3}{10}$
3.	$5\frac{7}{8}$ $-1\frac{3}{5}$	$3\frac{1}{9}$ $-\frac{1}{3}$	$2\frac{2}{3}$ $-1\frac{1}{2}$	$1\frac{3}{8}$ $-\frac{9}{10}$
4.	$4\frac{2}{9}$ $-\frac{2}{3}$	$6\frac{4}{5}$ $-5\frac{3}{7}$	$3\frac{7}{12}$ $-1\frac{9}{10}$	$2\frac{1}{8}$ $-\frac{5}{12}$

CHAPTER 13

Lesson 6 Problem Solving

Solve. Write each answer in simplest form.

1. One fish swam around the tank $1\frac{1}{2}$ times. Another swam around the tank $\frac{3}{4}$ of a time. How many more times around the tank did the first fish swim?

   It swam _____ time more around the tank.

   1.

2. Mrs. Tanner bought $2\frac{1}{2}$ cans of paint. She used $1\frac{2}{3}$ cans of paint on the garage. How much paint did she have left?

   She had _____ of a can left.

   2.

3. Lorena packed her overnight bag in $4\frac{1}{2}$ min. She packed the car in $1\frac{7}{10}$ min. How much longer did it take her to pack her bag than to pack the car?

   It took her _____ min longer to pack her bag.

   3.

4. Allen practised the guitar $1\frac{1}{4}$ h today. He practised $\frac{2}{3}$ h before lunch. How long did he practise after lunch?

   He practised _____ h after lunch.

   4.

5. Karen ran a race in $9\frac{3}{10}$ s. Curt ran the race in $7\frac{4}{5}$ s. How much longer did it take Karen to run the race?

   It took _____ s longer.

   5.

6. Fido can run the obstacle course in $2\frac{5}{8}$ min. Spot can run it in $2\frac{7}{9}$ min. How much faster can Fido run the race?

   Fido can run the race _____ min faster.

   6.

Lesson 7 Subtraction Review

Write each answer in simplest form.

	a	*b*	*c*	*d*

1.
$$\frac{7}{9} - \frac{4}{9}$$
$$\frac{7}{8} - \frac{1}{2}$$
$$\frac{7}{8} - \frac{3}{16}$$
$$\frac{11}{12} - \frac{1}{6}$$

2.
$$\frac{4}{5} - \frac{2}{3}$$
$$\frac{7}{10} - \frac{6}{10}$$
$$\frac{9}{10} - \frac{2}{5}$$
$$\frac{11}{12} - \frac{3}{4}$$

3.
$$\frac{5}{12} - \frac{3}{12}$$
$$\frac{3}{8} - \frac{1}{5}$$
$$\frac{5}{8} - \frac{3}{8}$$
$$\frac{2}{3} - \frac{1}{6}$$

4.
$$4\frac{7}{10} - 1\frac{2}{5}$$
$$3\frac{5}{12} - 1\frac{1}{12}$$
$$8\frac{3}{10} - 5\frac{9}{10}$$
$$5\frac{3}{8} - 3\frac{5}{8}$$

5.
$$1\frac{1}{4} - \frac{3}{10}$$
$$4\frac{6}{7} - 2\frac{3}{7}$$
$$1\frac{1}{3} - \frac{5}{6}$$
$$2\frac{4}{5} - \frac{9}{10}$$

Lesson 7 Problem Solving

Solve. Write each answer in simplest form.

1. Anne spends $9\frac{1}{4}$ h in bed each night. It takes her $\frac{3}{4}$ h
   to fall asleep. How long is she asleep each night?

   Anne is asleep for _____ h each night.

   | 1. |

2. Anne spends $6\frac{5}{8}$ h at school every day. She spends
   $1\frac{7}{8}$ h at lunch and recess. How long is she in class?

   Anne is in class for _____ h.

   | 2. |

3. John and Mara are reading the same book. John
   has read $\frac{4}{5}$ of the book and Mara has read $\frac{2}{3}$ of the
   book. How much more of the book has John read
   than Mara?

   John has read _____ more of the book.

   | 3. |

4. A frozen dinner calls for $3\frac{1}{2}$ min in the microwave
   on high and $1\frac{3}{4}$ min on medium. How much longer
   is the dinner on high than on medium?

   The dinner is on high for _____ min longer.

   | 4. |

5. Meagan worked $7\frac{1}{2}$ h. Joshua worked $5\frac{3}{4}$ h. How
   much longer than Joshua did Meagan work?

   She worked _____ h longer.

   | 5. |

6. It took Amber $2\frac{2}{3}$ h to read 2 books. She read one
   book in $\frac{5}{6}$ h. How long did it take her to read the
   other one?

   It took _____ h to read the other book.

   | 6. |

7. Mr. Wakefield used $8\frac{1}{4}$ buckets of water to fill two
   tanks. He put $3\frac{7}{8}$ buckets in one tank. How much
   water did he put in the other tank?

   He put _____ buckets in the other tank.

   | 7. |

Lesson 8 Subtraction Review

Write each answer in simplest form.

	a	*b*	*c*	*d*
1.	$\dfrac{7}{9}$ $-\dfrac{2}{9}$	$\dfrac{5}{7}$ $-\dfrac{1}{7}$	$\dfrac{5}{8}$ $-\dfrac{3}{8}$	$\dfrac{7}{10}$ $-\dfrac{1}{10}$
2.	$3\dfrac{5}{6}$ $-2\dfrac{1}{6}$	$4\dfrac{5}{9}$ $-3\dfrac{2}{9}$	$5\dfrac{1}{4}$ $-1\dfrac{3}{4}$	$1\dfrac{4}{15}$ $-\dfrac{7}{15}$
3.	$\dfrac{3}{4}$ $-\dfrac{2}{3}$	$\dfrac{4}{5}$ $-\dfrac{2}{3}$	$\dfrac{3}{4}$ $-\dfrac{1}{2}$	$\dfrac{5}{9}$ $-\dfrac{1}{3}$
4.	$\dfrac{7}{8}$ $-\dfrac{3}{4}$	$\dfrac{5}{6}$ $-\dfrac{1}{2}$	$\dfrac{3}{4}$ $-\dfrac{1}{6}$	$\dfrac{7}{10}$ $-\dfrac{1}{12}$
5.	$3\dfrac{7}{8}$ $-2\dfrac{1}{6}$	$4\dfrac{7}{10}$ $-1\dfrac{4}{5}$	$5\dfrac{5}{12}$ $-3\dfrac{7}{10}$	$6\dfrac{2}{9}$ $-\dfrac{11}{12}$

CHAPTER 13

Lesson 8 Problem Solving

In Allen's class, $\frac{1}{4}$ of the students have dogs, $\frac{1}{2}$ have cats, and $\frac{1}{8}$ have rabbits as pets.

Solve. Write each answer in simplest form.

1. What fraction more of the class have cats than dogs?

   _____ $\frac{1}{4}$ _____ more of the class have cats than dogs.

2. What fraction more of the class have dogs than rabbits?

   _____ $\frac{1}{8}$ _____ more of the class have dogs than rabbits.

3. What fraction more of the class have cats or rabbits than dogs?

   _____ $\frac{1}{2}$ _____ more of the class have cats or rabbits than dogs.

4. What fraction more of the class have none of these pets?

   _____ $\frac{1}{8}$ _____ of the class have none of these pets.

1.

2.

3.

4.

CHAPTER 13   PRACTICE TEST
Subtraction of Fractions

Write each answer in simplest form.

	a	*b*	*c*	*d*
1.	$\dfrac{9}{10}$ $-\dfrac{7}{10}$	$\dfrac{4}{5}$ $-\dfrac{2}{3}$	$\dfrac{3}{4}$ $-\dfrac{5}{8}$	$\dfrac{8}{9}$ $-\dfrac{2}{9}$
2.	$\dfrac{5}{6}$ $-\dfrac{1}{2}$	$\dfrac{1}{2}$ $-\dfrac{3}{8}$	$\dfrac{11}{12}$ $-\dfrac{3}{12}$	$\dfrac{1}{2}$ $-\dfrac{5}{12}$
3.	$\dfrac{3}{4}$ $-\dfrac{3}{8}$	$\dfrac{5}{6}$ $-\dfrac{1}{9}$	$\dfrac{7}{8}$ $-\dfrac{1}{4}$	$\dfrac{2}{3}$ $-\dfrac{1}{2}$
4.	$5\dfrac{7}{8}$ $-2\dfrac{3}{8}$	$4\dfrac{2}{5}$ $-2\dfrac{3}{10}$	$6\dfrac{1}{2}$ $-1\dfrac{1}{3}$	$3\dfrac{1}{3}$ $-1\dfrac{5}{6}$
5.	$3\dfrac{11}{12}$ $-1\dfrac{5}{6}$	$5\dfrac{5}{8}$ $-2\dfrac{3}{4}$	$2\dfrac{1}{9}$ $-\dfrac{7}{9}$	$1\dfrac{2}{5}$ $-\dfrac{1}{2}$

CHAPTER 14 PRETEST
Geometry

Circle the phrase that correctly describes each figure.

1. 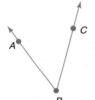 line *MN* line segment *MN* line *M*

2. line *R* line segment *RP* line *RP*

3.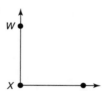

line segment *JK* ∥ line segment *LM*

line *JK* ⊥ line *LM*

line segment *JK* ⊥ line segment *LM*

4.

line *DE* ∥ line *FG*

line *DE* ⊥ line *FG*

line segment *DE* ∥ line segment *FG*

Name each angle. Give its measure and identify it as *acute*,
obtuse, or *right*.

5.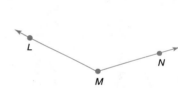

   a   *b*   *c*

_____ _____ _____

_____ _____ _____

Write the letter for the name of each figure in the blank.

    a   *b*

6. _____  _____

   a. octagon

   b. triangle

   c. hexagon

   d. pentagon

7. _____ _____

   e. square

   f. quadrilateral

   g. circle

Lesson 1 Lines and Line Segments

A **line** has no endpoints.

To name a line, name any two points on the line.

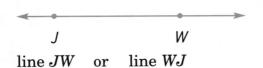

J   W

line *JW*   or   line *WJ*

A **line segment** has two **endpoints.**

A line segment is part of a line. The line segment consists of the endpoints and all points on the line between the endpoints. To name a line segment, name the endpoints.

G   S

line segment *GS*   or   line segment *SG*

Circle the correct name for each figure.

1.	line *AB*	line segment *BA*	line *CA*
2.	line segment *FG*	line *GF*	line *FG*
3.	line *CE*	line segment *CE*	line *CE*
4.	line segment *MN*	line *MN*	line *MN*
5.	line *RS*	line segment *RS*	line *SR*
6.	line segment *KI*	line *KI*	line *IK*
7.	line *XZ*	line segment *ZX*	line *ZX*
8.	line segment *PE*	line *EP*	line *EE*
9.	line *V*	line segment *VT*	line *VT*

Draw and label the following.

10. line segment *HQ*

Lesson 2 Parallel and Perpendicular

Parallel lines or line segments never intersect and are always the same distance apart. Parallel is indicated by the symbol ∥.

Use symbols to identify each figure.

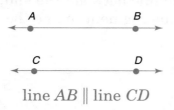

line *AB* ∥ line *CD*

Perpendicular lines or line segments intersect each other and form 90° angles. Perpendicular is indicated by the symbol ⊥.

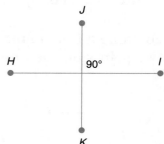

line segment *HI* ⊥ line segment *JK*

Use symbols to identify each figure.

a

b

1.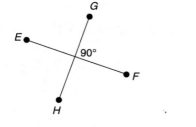

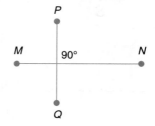

_____

_____

2.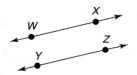

_____

_____

3.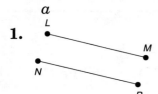

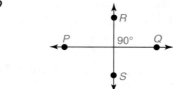

_____

_____

4.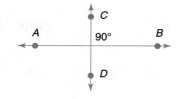

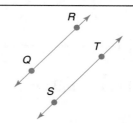

_____

_____

Lesson 3 Angles

An **angle** has two sides and a **vertex.**

Angle *GHB* (denoted ∠*GHB*) has a vertex of
H. When naming an angle, use the vertex
as the middle letter.

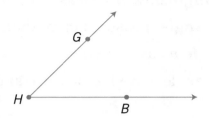

To use a protractor to measure an angle:

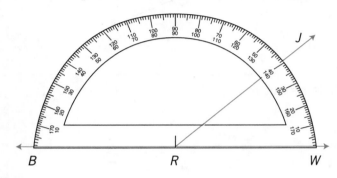

Place the centre of the protractor at the
vertex of the angle. Align one side of the
angle with the base of the protractor. Use
the scale starting at 0 and read the measure
of the angle.

The measurement of ∠*JRW* is 40°.
The measurement of ∠*JRB* is 140°.

Name each angle. Then use a protractor to measure each angle.

        a   *b*   *c*

1.   ∠___ ; ___°   ∠___ ; ___°

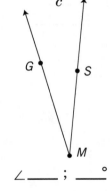

2.   ∠___ ; ___°

∠___ ; ___°

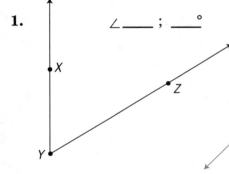

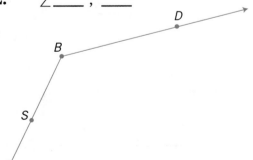

∠___ ; ___°

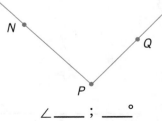

∠___ ; ___°

CHAPTER 14

Lesson 4 Acute, Obtuse, and Right Angles

An **acute angle** measures less than 90°.

An **obtuse angle** measures more than 90°.

A **right angle** measures 90°.

Name each angle. Give its measure and identify it as *acute, obtuse,* or *right.*

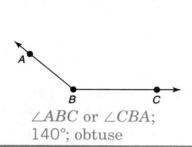

∠*ABC* or ∠*CBA*;
140°; obtuse

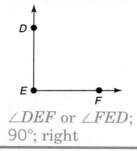

∠*DEF* or ∠*FED*;
90°; right

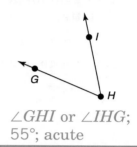

∠*GHI* or ∠*IHG*;
55°; acute

Name each angle. Give its measure and identify it as *acute, obtuse,* or *right.*

a	*b*	*c*

1.

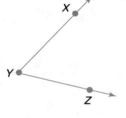

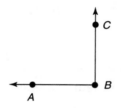

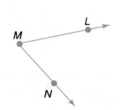

_____
_____

2.

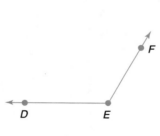

_____
_____

3.

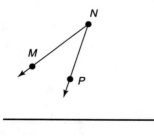

_____
_____

Lesson 5 Quadrilaterals

Quadrilaterals are figures that have four sides and four vertices. The following are more specific types of quadrilaterals.

| A **parallelogram** has two pairs of opposite sides that are parallel.  | A **rectangle** is a parallelogram with all right angles.  | A **square** is a rectangle with all sides the same length. |

A **trapezoid** has one pair of opposite sides that are parallel.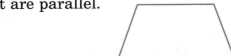

A **rhombus** is a parallelogram with all sides the same length.

Circle the name that best describes each quadrilateral.

1. 　　　square　　　trapezoid　　　parallelogram

2. 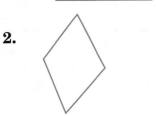　　　rectangle　　　square　　　rhombus

3. 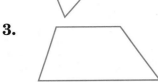　　　rhombus　　　trapezoid　　　parallelogram

4. 　　　square　　　parallelogram　　　rectangle

5. 　　　square　　　rhombus　　　rectangle

6. 　　　parallelogram　　　trapezoid　　　rectangle

CHAPTER 14

Lesson 6 Polygons

A **polygon** is a closed shape that is formed by three or more sides.
Polygons are named for the number of sides they have.

Triangle	**Quadrilateral**	**Pentagon**	**Hexagon**	**Heptagon**	**Octagon**
_3_ sides	___ sides	___ sides	___ sides	___ sides	___ sides

When all of the sides of a polygon are the same length, the
figure is called a **regular polygon**.

The figure to the right is a regular hexagon.

To name a polygon, use the letters of the vertices and list them
in alphabetical order.
The figure below is figure *ABCDE,* or pentagon *ABCDE.*

On the line after each name, write the letter(s) of the figure(s)
it describes. Some names will have more than one letter. Some
figures have more than one name.

1. pentagon _____

2. hexagon _____

3. octagon _____

4. triangle _____

5. heptagon _____

6. quadrilateral _____

7. regular triangle _____

8. regular hexagon _____

9. regular pentagon _____

10. regular quadrilateral _____

 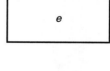 
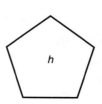

Lesson 6 Polygons

Name each figure shown.

a b c

11.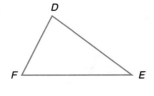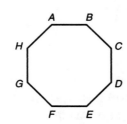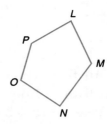

_____   _____   _____

12.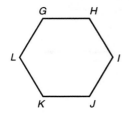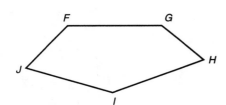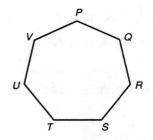

_____   _____   _____

A line segment that connects two vertices, but is not a side, is called a **diagonal.**

Two diagonals are drawn on pentagon *ABCDE*, diagonal *AD* and diagonal *EC*.

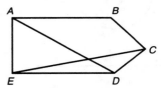

Draw and name all of the diagonals of each figure.

a b

13.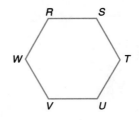

_____   _____

_____

Use problem **13** to answer the following questions.

14. Are all of the diagonals of figure *FGHIJ* the same length? _____

15. How many diagonals does figure *FGHIJ* have? _____

16. Are all of the diagonals of figure *RSTUVW* the same length? _____

17. How many diagonals does figure *RSTUVW* have? _____

CHAPTER 14

Lesson 7   Circles

To name a **circle,** use the letter at the centre of the circle.

Circle P

A line segment from the centre of the circle to any point on the circle is a **radius.** A line segment that has endpoints on the circle and passes through the centre of the circle is a **diameter.**

In circle L, LM is a radius and KN is a diameter.

Note that KL and LN are also **radii** (plural of radius).

Name each circle. Identify a radius and diameter of each circle.

| a | b | c |

1.

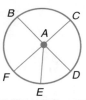

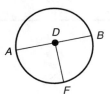

name: _____

radius: _____

_____

diameter: _____

name: _____

radius: _____

_____

diameter: _____

name: _____

radius: _____

_____

diameter: _____

2.

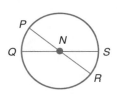

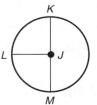

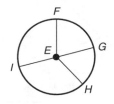

name: _____

radius: _____

_____

diameter: _____

name: _____

radius: _____

_____

diameter: _____

name: _____

radius: _____

_____

diameter: _____

3. Draw circle S with radius ST and diameter QR.

Lesson 8 Three-Dimensional Objects

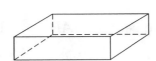
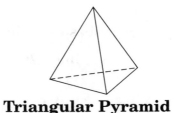
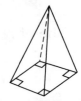

Cube　　　**Rectangular Prism**　　　**Triangular Pyramid**　　　**Square Pyramid**

Each of these objects has faces, edges, and vertices.
Each of the faces of these objects is a polygon.

This is a **face**.　　　This is an **edge**.　　　This is a **vertex**.

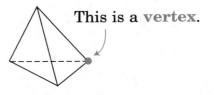

edge	face	rectangle	square	triangle	vertex
edges	faces	rectangles	squares	triangles	vertices

Choose from the list above to complete each sentence. You might use some words more than once. You might not use all the words.

1. All of the faces of a cube are _____.

2. All of the faces of a rectangular prism are _____.

3. The bottom face of a triangular pyramid is a _____.

4. The coloured part of object **A** below is a(n) _____.

5. The coloured part of object **B** below is a(n) _____.

6. The coloured part of object **C** below is a(n) _____.

A 　　　**B** 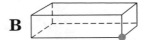　　　**C**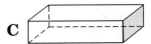

Answer each question with *Yes* or *No*.

7. Are all squares rectangles? _____

8. Are all faces of a cube rectangles? _____

9. Is a cube a rectangular prism? _____

CHAPTER 14   PRACTICE TEST
Geometry

Circle the phrase that correctly describes each figure.

1. 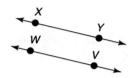   line *AB*   line segment *AB*   line *A*

2. 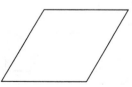   line *S*   line segment *ST*   line *ST*

3.   line segment *XY* ∥ line segment *WV*
line *XY* ∥ line *WV*
line segment *XY* ⊥ line segment *WV*

4.   line *FG* ∥ line *HJ*
line *FG* ⊥ line *HJ*
line segment *FG* ⊥ line segment *HJ*

Name each angle. Give its measure and identify it as *acute, obtuse,* or *right.*

        a   *b*   *c*

5.

_____   _____   _____

_____   _____   _____

Write the letter for the name of each figure in the blank.

      a   *b*

6. _____   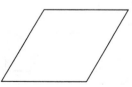   _____

      a. hexagon

      b. pentagon

      c. triangle

      d. heptagon

7. _____   _____

      e. circle

      f. quadrilateral

      g. octagon

MID-TEST Chapters 1–9

Solve each problem.

	a	*b*	*c*	*d*

1.

```
      4 2          9 2         1 3 4       4 6 8 2 1
    +5 1         +7 8        +9 3 9       9 3 2 8 9
                                        +2 5 3 9 4
```

2.

```
      7 5          2 3 6       1 0 4 3     3 5 6 7 0
    -1 8         -5 7        -3 8 9       -3 4 3 9 8
```

3.

```
      7 8          1 4 7         8 5 0       3 7 8 0
     ×5            ×9            ×8          ×1 0
```

4.

```
      3 7           9 2          2 4 8       1 5 6 9
    ×2 8          ×4 0          ×7 5        ×1 3 6
```

5.

```
6)9 6        8)9 8 4        9)3 1 9 8        7 3)7 3 3 8
```

Solve each problem.

	a	b	c	d
6.	5)92	4)248	49)1682	89)17 539
7.	14)98	9)186	81)2734	53)69 791

Estimate the answer to each problem.

	a	b	c	d
8.	78 +31	829 −377	68 ×3	5)241
9.	168 +511	7294 −867	684 ×17	7)4367

Solve each problem.

	a	b	c	d
10.	$3.75 +9.12	$5.18 −3.41	$4.29 ×5	5)$0.65
11.	$291.06 +88.64	$714.62 −126.33	$11.63 ×24	8)$75.04

MID-TEST   Chapters 1–9 (continued)

Use the bar graph to answer each question.

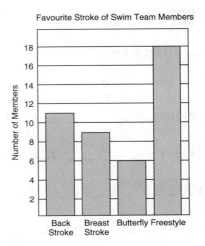

Favourite Stroke of Swim Team Members

12. How many members chose butterfly as their favourite stroke? _____

13. How many members chose freestyle as their favourite stroke? _____

14. How many more members chose back stroke as their favourite stroke than breast stroke? _____

Use the line graph to answer each question.

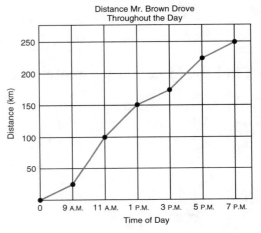

Distance Mr. Brown Drove Throughout the Day

15. How many kilometres did Mr. Brown drive by 9:00 A.M.? _____

16. How many kilometres did Mr. Brown drive by 5:00 P.M.? _____

17. By what time had Mr. Brown driven 150 km? _____

18. How many kilometres did Mr. Brown drive between 9:00 A.M. and 11:00 A.M.? _____

Find the mean, median, mode, and range of each set of numbers.

a

19. 2, 7, 4, 7, 5

mean: _____

median: _____

mode: _____

range: _____

b

33, 29, 45, 35, 36, 41, 33

mean: _____

median: _____

mode: _____

range: _____

20. 83%, 88%, 79%, 93%, 83%, 80%, 96%

mean: _____

median: _____

mode: _____

range: _____

$209, $218, $197, $224, $197

mean: _____

median: _____

mode: _____

range: _____

MID-TEST CH. 1–9

Complete the following.

a | b

21. 180 cm = _____ mm   3000 L = _____ kL

22. 21 g = _____ mg   300 kg = _____ g

23. 300 cm = _____ m   2 km = _____ m

24. 6 L = _____ mL   8 kg = _____ g

Find the area and perimeter of each figure.

a | b

25.

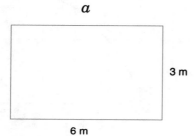
6 m · 3 m

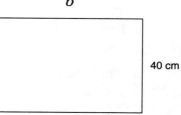
90 cm · 40 cm

perimeter: _____ m   *perimeter*: _____ cm

area: _____ m^2 *area*: _____ cm^2

Find the volume of each figure.

26.

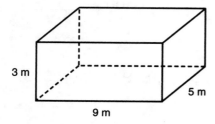
3 m · 9 m · 5 m

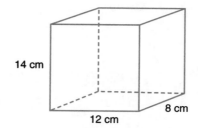
14 cm · 12 cm · 8 cm

volume: _____ m^3 *volume*: _____ cm^3

STOP

FINAL TEST   Chapters 1–14

Solve each problem.

	a	*b*	*c*	*d*

1.
```
     36        798      45 678      7 3 1 4
    +57       +135     +82 902      6 4 5 2
                                    9 7 1 5
                                    + 7 2 6
```

2.
```
     63        178       1270       59 246
    −18        −65       −982      −37 095
```

3.
```
     73        124        387        420
     ×6         ×8        ×10        ×32
```

4.
```
     36        657        526       2984
    ×27        ×89       ×154       ×697
```

5.   6)78   89)10 324   9)3729   51)6182

5.   5)97   4)231   45)935   93)27 658

Solve each problem.

	a	b	c	d
7.	$4.38 +1.07	$6.15 −3.82	$6.45 ×6	3)$0.81

8.	$379.25 +91.73	$843.26 −341.08	$21.18 ×32	7)$73.92

Find the mean, median, mode, and range of each set of numbers.

9.

a 13, 18, 11, 18, 15

mean: _____
median: _____
mode: _____
range: _____

b 65, 58, 46, 53, 49, 61, 46

mean: _____
median: _____
mode: _____
range: _____

Complete the following.

	a	*b*
10.	160 cm = _____ mm	6 km = _____ m
11.	17 L = _____ mL	9000 L = _____ kL
12.	9 g = _____ mg	30 kg = _____ g
13.	200 cm = _____ m	25 km = _____ m
14.	2 m = _____ mm	2 L = _____ mL
15.	3 L = _____ mL	6 kg = _____ g

GO ▶

Find the area and perimeter of each figure.

16.

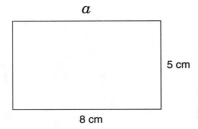

a

5 cm

8 cm

b

4 m

2 m

perimeter: _____ cm

area: _____ cm^2

perimeter: _____ m

area: _____ m^2

Change each fraction or mixed numeral to simplest form.

a	*b*	*c*	*d*	*e*
17. $\dfrac{9}{27} =$	$\dfrac{24}{30} =$	$\dfrac{35}{8} =$	$6\dfrac{4}{6} =$	$9\dfrac{16}{12} =$

Write each answer in simplest form.

a	*b*	*c*
18. $\dfrac{2}{3} \times \dfrac{1}{5} =$	$\dfrac{7}{8} \times \dfrac{1}{3} =$	$\dfrac{2}{7} \times \dfrac{3}{5} =$
19. $1\dfrac{1}{3} \times \dfrac{2}{5} =$	$\dfrac{3}{4} \times 2\dfrac{3}{6} =$	$3 \times \dfrac{5}{6} =$
20. $2\dfrac{1}{2} \times 3\dfrac{1}{3} =$	$\dfrac{7}{10} \times 5 =$	$4\dfrac{2}{5} \times 2\dfrac{3}{11} =$

a	*b*	*c*	*d*
21. $\dfrac{3}{5}$ $+\dfrac{1}{5}$	$\dfrac{2}{7}$ $+\dfrac{3}{7}$	$\dfrac{3}{10}$ $+\dfrac{3}{10}$	$1\dfrac{3}{8}$ $+2\dfrac{1}{8}$
22. $\dfrac{7}{8}$ $+\dfrac{1}{4}$	$\dfrac{5}{12}$ $+\dfrac{3}{4}$	$\dfrac{9}{10}$ $+\dfrac{2}{3}$	$12\dfrac{3}{4}$ $+9\dfrac{2}{3}$

GO ▶

Write each answer in simplest form.

	a	b	c	d

23.

$\begin{array}{r} \frac{7}{10} \\ -\frac{3}{10} \\ \hline \end{array}$
$\begin{array}{r} 7 \\ -\frac{3}{5} \\ \hline \end{array}$
$\begin{array}{r} 6\frac{3}{4} \\ -2\frac{1}{4} \\ \hline \end{array}$
$\begin{array}{r} \frac{7}{8} \\ -\frac{1}{4} \\ \hline \end{array}$

24.

$\begin{array}{r} 4\frac{7}{8} \\ -3\frac{2}{3} \\ \hline \end{array}$
$\begin{array}{r} 6\frac{9}{10} \\ -1\frac{7}{8} \\ \hline \end{array}$
$\begin{array}{r} \frac{11}{12} \\ -\frac{3}{4} \\ \hline \end{array}$
$\begin{array}{r} 9\frac{1}{4} \\ +6\frac{2}{5} \\ \hline \end{array}$

Name each figure.

25. <u>line AB</u>

26. <u>Obtuse angle DEF</u>

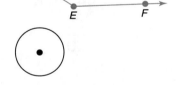

27. <u>Circle</u>

28. <u>pentagon</u>

29. <u>octogon</u>

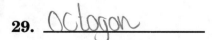

30. <u>square</u>

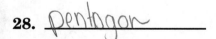

31. <u>triangle</u>

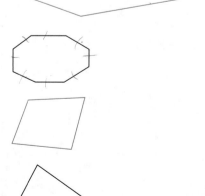

NAME _____

Do each problem.
Find the correct answer.
Mark the space for the answer.

Part 1 **Concepts**	Part 2 **Computation**

1. Which of the following addition problems has a sum closest to 500?

A 264 + 127
B 438 + 349
C 231 + 196
D 192 + 304

2. What is the estimated difference of 7819 − 4362?

A 3000
B 4000
C 5000
D 12 000

3. What number is in the hundreds place in the sum of 6804 + 559?

A 3
B 5
C 6
D 7

4. Which of the following statements is true about the difference of 24 581 and 15 216?

A The difference is greater than 10 000.
B The difference is less than 9000.
C The difference is an even number.
D The difference is an odd number.

5. 92
      −67

A 159   C 35
B 25   D 27

6. 718
      +425

A 293   C 1143
B 1133   D 393

7. 6219
      −3468

A 2751
B 9687
C 3851
D 3741

8. 8164
      +5457

A 40 725
B 13 511
C 2707
D 13 621

9. 149 127
      −64 853

A 203 970
B 84 274
C 185 374
D 184 273

10. 41 002
       −18 653

A 25 001
B 25 351
C 22 349
D 59 655

GO

ANSWER ROW **1** Ⓐ Ⓑ Ⓒ Ⓓ   **3** Ⓐ Ⓑ Ⓒ Ⓓ   **5** Ⓐ Ⓑ Ⓒ Ⓓ   **7** Ⓐ Ⓑ Ⓒ Ⓓ   **9** Ⓐ Ⓑ Ⓒ Ⓓ
                    2 Ⓐ Ⓑ Ⓒ Ⓓ   **4** Ⓐ Ⓑ Ⓒ Ⓓ   **6** Ⓐ Ⓑ Ⓒ Ⓓ   **8** Ⓐ Ⓑ Ⓒ Ⓓ   **10** Ⓐ Ⓑ Ⓒ Ⓓ

11.

381	A	1363
945	B	1466
+137	C	1463
	D	1353

12.

3507	A	24 336
9124	B	25 446
7635	C	26 346
+5180	D	15 447

Part 3 **Applications**

13. Casey rode his bike 18 km on Saturday and 24 km on Sunday. How many more kilometres did Casey ride his bike on Sunday?

A 42   c 16

B 7   D 6

14. On Monday, Joslyn read 24 pages of her book. On Tuesday, she read 37 pages of her book. On Wednesday, she read 33 pages of her book. How many total pages did Joslyn read on Monday, Tuesday, and Wednesday?

A 61   c 84

B 94   D 105

15. On Friday, Mr. Carmona drove 327 km. On Saturday, he drove 189 km. Use estimation to determine the approximate number of kilometres Mr. Carmona drove on Friday and Saturday.

A 300   c 500

B 600   D 400

16. Luisa and Jeff both flew to separate cities for business trips. Luisa's flight was 184 min long. Jeff's flight was 127 min long. How many minutes longer was Luisa's flight?

A 211   c 47

B 201   D 57

17. For a fundraiser at school, students were selling chocolate bars. Amber sold 49 chocolate bars, Carlton sold 57 chocolate bars, and Takara sold 61 chocolate bars. Altogether, how many chocolate bars did Amber, Carlton, and Takara sell?

A 157   c 127

B 167   D 166

18. In 1990, the population of a small town was 16 843. In 2000, the population of the same town was 22 058. How much greater was the population in the year 2000 than in 1990?

A 5215   c 38 901

B 38 891 D 5415

STOP

ANSWER ROW **11** Ⓐ Ⓑ Ⓒ Ⓓ **13** Ⓐ Ⓑ Ⓒ Ⓓ **15** Ⓐ Ⓑ Ⓒ Ⓓ **17** Ⓐ Ⓑ Ⓒ Ⓓ
12 Ⓐ Ⓑ Ⓒ Ⓓ **14** Ⓐ Ⓑ Ⓒ Ⓓ **16** Ⓐ Ⓑ Ⓒ Ⓓ **18** Ⓐ Ⓑ Ⓒ Ⓓ

CHAPTER 2   CUMULATIVE REVIEW

Do each problem.
Find the correct answer.
Mark the space for the answer.

| Part 1 **Concepts** | Part 2 **Computation** |

1. What number is in the tens place in the product of 34 and 43?

   A 1   C 4

   B 2   D 6

2. Which of the following products is the greatest?

   A 34×9 C 49×5

   B 18×15 D 68×4

3. Which problem would you use to find the estimated sum of 5789 and 8203?

   A $6000 + 9000$ C $5000 + 8000$

   B $6000 + 8000$ D $5700 + 8200$

4. What is the estimated product of 382 and 831?

   A 240 000   C 320 000

   B 360 000   D 270 000

5. What is the product of 15 and 153?

   A 2295   C 1295

   B 2150   D 4235

6.
$$\begin{array}{r} 53 \\ +32 \\ \hline \end{array}$$

   A 21

   B 75

   C 32

   D 85

7.
$$\begin{array}{r} 635 \\ -172 \\ \hline \end{array}$$

   A 807

   B 463

   C 707

   D 563

8.
$$\begin{array}{r} 2834 \\ -368 \\ \hline \end{array}$$

   A 2496

   B 2466

   C 3202

   D 2576

9.
$$\begin{array}{r} 8395 \\ +3705 \\ \hline \end{array}$$

   A 12 100

   B 5680

   C 4690

   D 11 090

10.
$$\begin{array}{r} 869 \\ 432 \\ 257 \\ +118 \\ \hline \end{array}$$

   A 1556

   B 1664

   C 1766

   D 1676

CUMULATIVE REVIEW

ANSWER ROW **1** Ⓐ Ⓑ Ⓒ Ⓓ **3** Ⓐ Ⓑ Ⓒ Ⓓ **5** Ⓐ Ⓑ Ⓒ Ⓓ **7** Ⓐ Ⓑ Ⓒ Ⓓ **9** Ⓐ Ⓑ Ⓒ Ⓓ

              2 Ⓐ Ⓑ Ⓒ Ⓓ **4** Ⓐ Ⓑ Ⓒ Ⓓ **6** Ⓐ Ⓑ Ⓒ Ⓓ **8** Ⓐ Ⓑ Ⓒ Ⓓ **10** Ⓐ Ⓑ Ⓒ Ⓓ

11. 64
       ×5

A 320
B 119
C 69
D 300

12. 53
       ×21

A 814
B 1103
C 1113
D 159

13. 827
       ×60

A 48 220
B 15 757
C 50 220
D 49 620

14. 416
       ×209

A 85 894
B 86 944
C 4576
D 86 953

Part 3 Applications

15. On a reading test, there were three sections. The number of points earned from each section is added together to get each test score. Marcy scored 38 points on the multiple choice section, 22 points on the matching section, and 31 points on the essay section. What was Marcy's test score?

A 81   C 91
B 90   D Not Given

16. Attendance at a high school basketball game for two consecutive games was 372 and 415. What was the difference in the attendance for these two games?

A 787   C 35
B 163   D 43

17. There are six buses taking students on a field trip to the zoo. Each bus is carrying 76 students. How many students are going on the field trip?

A 426   C 82
B 456   D 526

18. Emily's car can go 426 km on one tank of gas. How many kilometres can her car go on 13 tanks of gas?

A 439   C 5428
B 6129   D Not Given

19. There are 34 rows of seats in the auditorium. Each row has 16 seats. How many seats are in the auditorium?

A 544   C 50
B 550   D 524

20. There are 168 h in one week. How many hours are there in 52 weeks?

A 7620   C 8736
B 220   D 5226

STOP

ANSWER ROW **11** Ⓐ Ⓑ Ⓒ Ⓓ **13** Ⓐ Ⓑ Ⓒ Ⓓ **15** Ⓐ Ⓑ Ⓒ Ⓓ **17** Ⓐ Ⓑ Ⓒ Ⓓ **19** Ⓐ Ⓑ Ⓒ Ⓓ
                  12 Ⓐ Ⓑ Ⓒ Ⓓ **14** Ⓐ Ⓑ Ⓒ Ⓓ **16** Ⓐ Ⓑ Ⓒ Ⓓ **18** Ⓐ Ⓑ Ⓒ Ⓓ **20** Ⓐ Ⓑ Ⓒ Ⓓ

NAME _____

Do each problem.
Find the correct answer.
Mark the space for the answer.

| Part 1 **Concepts** | Part 2 **Computation** |

1. Which of the following subtraction problems has a difference closest to 200?

 A 648 − 315   C 591 − 471
 B 918 − 725   D 784 − 507

2. What number is in the hundreds place in the sum of 6734 and 4318?

 A 0   C 1
 B 1   D 5

3. Which problem would you use to find the estimated product of 89 and 104?

 A 80 × 100   C 90 × 110
 B 90 × 100   D 80 × 110

4. Which of the following division problems has the greatest quotient?

 A 8)272   C 5)185
 B 4)132   D 9)288

5. Which problem would you use to find the estimated product of 593 and 287?

 A 600 × 300   C 590 × 280
 B 500 × 200   D 600 × 200

6. 76
  −34

 A 100
 B 42
 C 110
 D 44

7. 614
  +237

 A 487
 B 841
 C 377
 D 851

8. 21 763
  −9 885

 A 11 878
 B 22 988
 C 31 648
 D 12 988

9. 819
  ×6

 A 4923
 B 1485
 C 4914
 D 4864

10. 653
  ×847

 A 12 407
 B 1500
 C 544 191
 D 553 091

GO ▶

CUMULATIVE REVIEW

ANSWER ROW **1** Ⓐ Ⓑ Ⓒ Ⓓ **3** Ⓐ Ⓑ Ⓒ Ⓓ **5** Ⓐ Ⓑ Ⓒ Ⓓ **7** Ⓐ Ⓑ Ⓒ Ⓓ **9** Ⓐ Ⓑ Ⓒ Ⓓ
     2 Ⓐ Ⓑ Ⓒ Ⓓ **4** Ⓐ Ⓑ Ⓒ Ⓓ **6** Ⓐ Ⓑ Ⓒ Ⓓ **8** Ⓐ Ⓑ Ⓒ Ⓓ **10** Ⓐ Ⓑ Ⓒ Ⓓ

11. $4\overline{)72}$

    A 17 r2   C 108

    B 18   D 19

12. $8\overline{)658}$

    A 82 r2   C 79 r7

    B 81   D 93 r4

13. $9\overline{)2349}$

    A 262   C 272 r1

    B 334 r3   D 261

14. $7\overline{)95}$

    A 10 r5   C 13 r4

    B 13   D 14 r3

15. $5\overline{)648}$

    A 132   C 125 r3

    B 129 r3   D 29

Part 3 Applications

16. Kaya has 456 stickers in her sticker collection. Shanice has 507 stickers in her sticker collection. Together, how many stickers do Kaya and Shanice have in their sticker collections?

    A 952   C 151

    B 963   D 1063

17. In one year, Mrs. Wessel drove her personal car 8541 km and she drove her business car 13 083 km. How many more kilometres did Mrs. Wessel drive her company car?

    A 5543   C 21 624

    B 4632   D 4542

18. In the soccer league, there are eight teams with 17 members on each team. How many members are in the soccer league?

    A 105   C 134

    B 136   D 143

19. The grocery store received 23 boxes that contain cans of soup. Each box contains 48 cans of soup. How many cans of soup did the grocery store receive?

    A 240   C 1104

    B 1312   D 71

20. Each of the 23 students in Mr. Perez's class sold the same number of chocolate bars for a school fundraiser. Mr. Perez's class sold a total of 621 chocolate bars. How many chocolate bars did each student in Mr. Perez's class sell?

    A 22   C 23

    B 25   D 27

STOP

ANSWER ROW **11** Ⓐ Ⓑ Ⓒ Ⓓ **13** Ⓐ Ⓑ Ⓒ Ⓓ **15** Ⓐ Ⓑ Ⓒ Ⓓ **17** Ⓐ Ⓑ Ⓒ Ⓓ **19** Ⓐ Ⓑ Ⓒ Ⓓ

                12 Ⓐ Ⓑ Ⓒ Ⓓ **14** Ⓐ Ⓑ Ⓒ Ⓓ **16** Ⓐ Ⓑ Ⓒ Ⓓ **18** Ⓐ Ⓑ Ⓒ Ⓓ **20** Ⓐ Ⓑ Ⓒ Ⓓ

NAME _____

Do each problem.
Find the correct answer.
Mark the space for the answer.

Part 1 Concepts

1. Which of the following products is the smallest?

A 168×23 C 93×45

B 71×64 D 108×36

2. What number is in the thousands place in the answer to the problem of $34\,081 + 18\,765$?

A   5   C   2

B   4   D   8

3. What is the remainder of the division problem $8\overline{)371}$?

A   2   C   4

B   3   D   6

4. Which of the following division problems does not have a remainder?

A $15\overline{)943}$ C $37\overline{)6913}$

B $26\overline{)846}$ D $85\overline{)9435}$

Part 2 Computation

5.   4348
       $+912$

A   4436   C   5260

B   4250   D   3436

6.   5906
       -2182

A   3724   C   3824

B   7088   D   8088

7.   24
       $\times 36$

A   660   C   60

B   7344   D   864

8. $7\overline{)99}$

A   14   C   14 r1

B   12   D   12 r5

9. $5\overline{)805}$

A   141   C   159

B   161   D   181

10. $7\overline{)896}$

A   132   C   128

B   144   D   235

GO ➡

ANSWER ROW   **1** Ⓐ Ⓑ Ⓒ Ⓓ   **3** Ⓐ Ⓑ Ⓒ Ⓓ   **5** Ⓐ Ⓑ Ⓒ Ⓓ   **7** Ⓐ Ⓑ Ⓒ Ⓓ   **9** Ⓐ Ⓑ Ⓒ Ⓓ

                 2 Ⓐ Ⓑ Ⓒ Ⓓ   **4** Ⓐ Ⓑ Ⓒ Ⓓ   **6** Ⓐ Ⓑ Ⓒ Ⓓ   **8** Ⓐ Ⓑ Ⓒ Ⓓ   **10** Ⓐ Ⓑ Ⓒ Ⓓ

11. 15)621

A 41 r6
B 41
C 56 r11
D 41 r5

12. 27)729

A 34 r11
B 27 r20
C 27
D 21 r19

13. 71)1474

A 30 r44
B 20 r54
C 19 r25
D 21 r8

Part 3 Applications

14. There are 148 pages in Antwan's new book. He has read 85 pages. How many pages does he have left to read?

A 68　　　C 70
B 63　　　D 85

15. The populations of four cities are 72 369, 69 516, 67 842, and 71 096. What is the total population of all four cities?

A 209 727　　　C 279 422
B 280 823　　　D 380 823

17. Each box of cereal has a mass of 450 g. What is the total mass of 8 boxes?

A 4500 g　　　C 4200 g
B 690 g　　　D 3600 g

17. The airline distance between two cities is 462 km. How many kilometres would an airplane travel in making 34 one-way trips?

A 14 708　　　C 15 708
B 15 608　　　D 15 508

18. There are 115 students in grade 5 at Middletown Elementary School. There are five different classrooms with the same number of students in each. How many students are in each classroom?

A 23　　　C 29
B 25　　　D 21

19. Six students shared the cost of a weekend camping trip. If the total cost of the trip was $348, what was each student's share?

A $116　　　C $48
B $58　　　D $34

20. A machine operated for 48 h and produced 8016 parts. The same number of parts were produced each hour. How many parts were produced each hour?

A 4008　　　C 159
B 248　　　D 167

ANSWER ROW **11** Ⓐ Ⓑ Ⓒ Ⓓ　**13** Ⓐ Ⓑ Ⓒ Ⓓ　**15** Ⓐ Ⓑ Ⓒ Ⓓ　**17** Ⓐ Ⓑ Ⓒ Ⓓ　**19** Ⓐ Ⓑ Ⓒ Ⓓ
　　　　　　12 Ⓐ Ⓑ Ⓒ Ⓓ　**14** Ⓐ Ⓑ Ⓒ Ⓓ　**16** Ⓐ Ⓑ Ⓒ Ⓓ　**18** Ⓐ Ⓑ Ⓒ Ⓓ　**20** Ⓐ Ⓑ Ⓒ Ⓓ

NAME _____

Do each problem.
Find the correct answer.
Mark the space for the answer.

Part 1 Concepts

1. What is the sum of eighty-three and fifty-nine?

A 132   C 112
B 4897   D 142

2. What digit is in the hundreds place in the difference of 4703 and 2576?

A 3   C 2
B 0   D 1

3. What is the remainder of the division problem $21\overline{)947}$?

A 2   C 4
B 9   D 21

4. What number is the dividend in the problem $85\overline{)5307}$?

A 62   C 85
B 5306   D 36

5. What number is the divisor in the problem $46\overline{)989}$?

A 989   C 20
B 21   D 46

Part 2 Computation

6.   36
        +57

A 83
B 93
C 94
D 103

7. 17 362
        −9 548

A 7814
B 8814
C 7824
D 7816

8.   45
        ×16

A 690
B 720
C 29
D 72

9. $6\overline{)84}$

A 24
B 504
C 18
D 14

10. $5\overline{)4106}$

A 821 r6
B 802 r1
C 821 r1
D 820 r6

ANSWER ROW   **1** Ⓐ Ⓑ Ⓒ Ⓓ   **3** Ⓐ Ⓑ Ⓒ Ⓓ   **5** Ⓐ Ⓑ Ⓒ Ⓓ   **7** Ⓐ Ⓑ Ⓒ Ⓓ   **9** Ⓐ Ⓑ Ⓒ Ⓓ
             2 Ⓐ Ⓑ Ⓒ Ⓓ   **4** Ⓐ Ⓑ Ⓒ Ⓓ   **6** Ⓐ Ⓑ Ⓒ Ⓓ   **8** Ⓐ Ⓑ Ⓒ Ⓓ   **10** Ⓐ Ⓑ Ⓒ Ⓓ

11. $12\overline{)3000}$

    A 250
    B 25
    C 205
    D 600

12. $34\overline{)850}$

    A 25 r20
    B 25
    C 27 r32
    D 816

13. $73\overline{)4161}$

    A 4088
    B 67
    C 57
    D 61

14. $47\overline{)35\,918}$

    A 792 r4
    B 753
    C 764 r4
    D 764 r10

Part 3 Applications

15. The number of parts shipped to three different countries was 671, 818, and 448. How many parts were shipped in all?

    A 1927   C 1937
    B 1837   D 1827

16. It takes Samantha 18 min to run around the lake. How many minutes will it take Samantha to run around the lake four times?

    A 22   C 60
    B 54   D 72

17. A factory shipped 858 tires to six different cities. Each city received the same number of tires. How many tires did each city receive?

    A 142   C 134
    B 143   D 192

18. In Section C of an arena, there are 450 seats. Each row has 18 seats. How many rows are in Section C?

    A 25   C 35
    B 8100   D 7100

19. There are 2941 potatoes to be put into bags. Each bag will contain 17 potatoes. How many bags will be needed?

    A 2924   C 17
    B 183   D 173

20. During 3 months, 93 employees worked 42 408 h. Each employee worked the same number of hours. How many hours did each employee work during the 3 months?

    A 456   C 14 136
    B 279   D 269

STOP

ANSWER ROW   **11** Ⓐ Ⓑ Ⓒ Ⓓ   **13** Ⓐ Ⓑ Ⓒ Ⓓ   **15** Ⓐ Ⓑ Ⓒ Ⓓ   **17** Ⓐ Ⓑ Ⓒ Ⓓ   **19** Ⓐ Ⓑ Ⓒ Ⓓ
           12 Ⓐ Ⓑ Ⓒ Ⓓ   **14** Ⓐ Ⓑ Ⓒ Ⓓ   **16** Ⓐ Ⓑ Ⓒ Ⓓ   **18** Ⓐ Ⓑ Ⓒ Ⓓ   **20** Ⓐ Ⓑ Ⓒ Ⓓ

PRISM MATHEMATICS
Yellow Book

CHAPTER 5
CUMULATIVE REVIEW

226

CHAPTER 6 CUMULATIVE REVIEW

Do each problem.
Find the correct answer.
Mark the space for the answer.

Part 1 Concepts

1. Which of the following products is the greatest?

  A 46 × 49   C 33 × 65

  B 29 × 87   D 72 × 18

2. What number is the divisor in the problem 34)7438?

  A 7438   C 34

  B 218   D 26

3. What number is in the hundredths place in $1529.74?

  A 5   C 7

  B 2   D 4

4. Write $924.08 using words.

  A nine twenty-four and eight tenths

  B nine hundred twenty-four dollars and eighty cents

  C nine hundred twenty-four dollars and eight cents

  D ninety-two dollars and eight cents

5. What number is in the ones place in $538.29?

  A 8   C 5

  B 9   D 3

Part 2 Computation

6.
$$\begin{array}{r} 798 \\ +135 \\ \hline \end{array}$$

  A 923

  B 933

  C 833

  D 823

7.
$$\begin{array}{r} 1270 \\ -982 \\ \hline \end{array}$$

  A 2252

  B 298

  C 398

  D 288

8.
$$\begin{array}{r} 614 \\ \times 53 \\ \hline \end{array}$$

  A 32 542

  B 4912

  C 31 542

  D 30 542

9. 3)741

  A 271

  B 247

  C 410

  D 120

10. 63)2923

  A 40 r3

  B 46 r35

  C 46 r63

  D 46 r25

CUMULATIVE REVIEW

GO

ANSWER ROW   **1** Ⓐ Ⓑ Ⓒ Ⓓ   **3** Ⓐ Ⓑ Ⓒ Ⓓ   **5** Ⓐ Ⓑ Ⓒ Ⓓ   **7** Ⓐ Ⓑ Ⓒ Ⓓ   **9** Ⓐ Ⓑ Ⓒ Ⓓ

                  2 Ⓐ Ⓑ Ⓒ Ⓓ   **4** Ⓐ Ⓑ Ⓒ Ⓓ   **6** Ⓐ Ⓑ Ⓒ Ⓓ   **8** Ⓐ Ⓑ Ⓒ Ⓓ   **10** Ⓐ Ⓑ Ⓒ Ⓓ

11. 15)‾1470

A 90 r8
B 90 r12
C 98
D 90

12. $84.23
−61.94

A $23.29
B $22.29
C $146.17
D $157.18

13. $52.25
×6

A $313.20
B $3135.00
C $118.91
D $313.50

14. 8)‾$11.92

A $1.49
B $1.47
C $1.39
D $1.52

Part 3 Applications

15. Mr. Allen had 86 963 km on his car at the end of January. By the end of February, he had 88 042 km on his car. How many kilometres did Mr. Allen drive his car in February?

A 2198
C 1079
B 88 042
D 1457

16. A truck driver is delivering boxes of books to schools. Each box contains 12 books. He delivers 25 boxes to one school. How many books did he deliver to that school?

A 300
C 275
B 12
D 13

17. There are 93 elementary school classrooms in the Plainsville School District. These classrooms hold 2604 students. Each classroom has the same number of students. How many students are there in each classroom?

A 30
C 32
B 28
D 23

18. A carton holds 24 cans of juice. How many cartons will it take to hold 1512 cans?

A 60
C 71
B 63
D 80

19. Mrs. Anderson spent $73.95 at the grocery store. She gave the cashier $80.00. How much change did Mrs. Anderson get back?

A $7.15
C $6.05
B $153.95
D $5.55

20. Ben and four of his friends ordered pizzas. The bill came to $19.00. They split the bill evenly among all of them. How much did each boy pay?

A $3.80
C $95.00
B $4.75
D $3.17

ANSWER ROW **11** Ⓐ Ⓑ Ⓒ Ⓓ **13** Ⓐ Ⓑ Ⓒ Ⓓ **15** Ⓐ Ⓑ Ⓒ Ⓓ **17** Ⓐ Ⓑ Ⓒ Ⓓ **19** Ⓐ Ⓑ Ⓒ Ⓓ
12 Ⓐ Ⓑ Ⓒ Ⓓ **14** Ⓐ Ⓑ Ⓒ Ⓓ **16** Ⓐ Ⓑ Ⓒ Ⓓ **18** Ⓐ Ⓑ Ⓒ Ⓓ **20** Ⓐ Ⓑ Ⓒ Ⓓ

NAME _____

Do each problem.
Find the correct answer.
Mark the space for the answer.

Part 1 Concepts

1. Which problem would you use to find the estimated difference of 831 and 483?

  A   800 − 400   c   900 − 400

  B   800 − 500   D   900 − 500

2. Which of the following dollar amounts has a 4 in the tenths place?

  A $926.45   c $308.64

  B $754.91   D $145.07

3. Which of the following words means "the middle number"?

  A   median   c   range

  B   mode   D   mean

4. Which of the following means the number that appears most often in a set of numbers?

  A   median   c   range

  B   mode   D   mean

5. Which of the following words means the chance that something will occur?

  A   mode   c   median

  B   range   D   probability

Part 2 Computation

6.
$$\begin{array}{r} 1356 \\ 793 \\ +2684 \\ \hline \end{array}$$

  A   3833

  B   4833

  c   4823

  D   4723

7.
$$\begin{array}{r} 754 \\ \times 32 \\ \hline \end{array}$$

  A   24 028

  B   23 128

  c   24 128

  D   23 028

8. $6\overline{)3892}$

  A   640 r5

  B   644 r4

  c   650 r5

  D   648 r4

9. $45\overline{)3150}$

  A   7

  B   31

  c   70

  D   75

10. $61\overline{)7285}$

  A   119 r2

  B   119 r42

  c   119 r34

  D   119 r43

GO

ANSWER ROW   **1** Ⓐ Ⓑ Ⓒ Ⓓ   **3** Ⓐ Ⓑ Ⓒ Ⓓ   **5** Ⓐ Ⓑ Ⓒ Ⓓ   **7** Ⓐ Ⓑ Ⓒ Ⓓ   **9** Ⓐ Ⓑ Ⓒ Ⓓ

                2 Ⓐ Ⓑ Ⓒ Ⓓ   **4** Ⓐ Ⓑ Ⓒ Ⓓ   **6** Ⓐ Ⓑ Ⓒ Ⓓ   **8** Ⓐ Ⓑ Ⓒ Ⓓ   **10** Ⓐ Ⓑ Ⓒ Ⓓ

11. $452.35
+986.54

   A $1506.65   C $1439.89
   B $1438.89   D $1338.90

12. $913.55
−639.12

   A $374.43   C $274.43
   B $293.42   D $294.43

13. $3.47
×12

   A $41.74   C $41.77
   B $40.64   D $41.64

14. What is the mean of 11, 16, 9, 13, and 11?

   A 7   C 11
   B 12   D 10

15. A number cube has sides labelled A, B, C, D, E, and F. What is the probability of rolling an E?

   A $\frac{1}{3}$ C $\frac{1}{6}$
   B $\frac{1}{2}$ D $\frac{1}{5}$

Part 3 Applications

16. On Monday, Shontay drove 293 km. On Tuesday, she drove 137 km. How many more kilometres did Shontay drive on Monday than on Tuesday?

   A 430   C 137
   B 146   D 156

17. Maggie bought 6 T-shirts. Each T-shirt cost $13.75. How much money did Maggie spend on the T-shirts?

   A $82.50   C $68.50
   B $78.50   D $78.20

18. There are 894 boxes ready to be shipped. Only 38 boxes will fit in each truck. How many trucks will be needed to ship all the boxes?

   A 23   C 38
   B 20   D 24

19. Kenji, Sarah, Felix, and Darnell spent 3 h on Saturday raking leaves. They were paid $22.00. They split the money evenly among them. How much money did each receive?

   A $7.34   C $5.50
   B $12.00   D $7.50

Use this graph to answer question **20.**

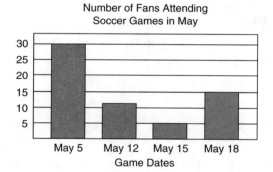

Number of Fans Attending Soccer Games in May

20. How many more fans attended the May 5 game than the May 15 game?

   A 15   C 19
   B 25   D 23

STOP

ANSWER ROW **11** Ⓐ Ⓑ Ⓒ Ⓓ   **13** Ⓐ Ⓑ Ⓒ Ⓓ   **15** Ⓐ Ⓑ Ⓒ Ⓓ   **17** Ⓐ Ⓑ Ⓒ Ⓓ   **19** Ⓐ Ⓑ Ⓒ Ⓓ
              12 Ⓐ Ⓑ Ⓒ Ⓓ   **14** Ⓐ Ⓑ Ⓒ Ⓓ   **16** Ⓐ Ⓑ Ⓒ Ⓓ   **18** Ⓐ Ⓑ Ⓒ Ⓓ   **20** Ⓐ Ⓑ Ⓒ Ⓓ

NAME _____

Do each problem.
Find the correct answer.
Mark the space for the answer.

Part 1 Concepts

1. What digit is <u>in the ones place</u> in the quotient of 14)2567?

   A   4   C   3
   B   7   D   5

2. Which of the following sums is the greatest?

   A $839.73 + 274.11
   B $438.27 + 728.10
   C $910.35 + 183.49
   D $602.76 + 538.27

3. Which of the following means the difference between the greatest and least number in a set of numbers?

   A   mean   C   mode
   B   median   D   range

4. Which of the following units of measure could represent the length of a room?

   A   13 L   C   5 m
   B   13 kg   D   5 g

5. Which of the following products is the smallest?

   A 65×14 C 114×10
   B 181×8 D 88×57

Part 2 Computation

6.
   3067
  −1372

   A   1745
   B   1695
   C   2695
   D   1795

7.
  354
  ×7

   A   2458
   B   2178
   C   2478
   D   2358

8. 8)89

   A   10 r1
   B   11 r1
   C   9 r8
   D   8 r1

9. 24)$39.12

   A $1.63
   B $1.12
   C $1.36
   D $1.53

10.
  $839.46
  +173.45

   A $1042.91
   B $942.81
   C $1042.81
   D $1012.91

CUMULATIVE REVIEW

ANSWER ROW   **1** Ⓐ Ⓑ Ⓒ Ⓓ   **3** Ⓐ Ⓑ Ⓒ Ⓓ   **5** Ⓐ Ⓑ Ⓒ Ⓓ   **7** Ⓐ Ⓑ Ⓒ Ⓓ   **9** Ⓐ Ⓑ Ⓒ Ⓓ
               2 Ⓐ Ⓑ Ⓒ Ⓓ   **4** Ⓐ Ⓑ Ⓒ Ⓓ   **6** Ⓐ Ⓑ Ⓒ Ⓓ   **8** Ⓐ Ⓑ Ⓒ Ⓓ   **10** Ⓐ Ⓑ Ⓒ Ⓓ

11. What is the mode of 46, 38, 36, 31, 47, 32, and 36?

A   31   C   38
B   36   D   16

12. 6 cm = _____ mm

A   6   C   60
B   600   D   6000

13. 5000 mg = _____ g

A   5   C   50
B   500   D   5 000 000

14. What is the perimeter of the figure shown?

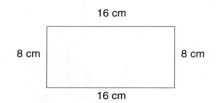

A   40 cm   C   128 cm
B   48 cm   D   64 cm

Part 3 Applications

15. Marcus rode his bike four days this week. Monday he biked 15 km. Wednesday he biked 9 km. Thursday he biked 13 km. Saturday he biked 21 km. How many kilometres did Marcus bike this week?

A   50   C   58
B   48   D   40

16. Jennifer works 17 h each week at her part-time job. How many hours does Jennifer work in 4 weeks at her part-time job?

A   42   C   34
B   68   D   51

17. Your school is having a car wash to raise money for a local charity. You charge $3.50 for each car you wash. If you wash 57 cars, how much money will your school raise?

A $199.50   C $85.50
B $171.50   D $175.00

18. Paul has five $5 bills, three $10 bills, and two $20 bills in his wallet. Without looking, Paul selects one bill from his wallet. What is the probability Paul selected a $5 bill?

A $\frac{1}{5}$ C $\frac{3}{10}$

B $\frac{1}{2}$ D $\frac{1}{8}$

19. Maya is buying new carpet for her bedroom. Her bedroom is 12 m by 13 m. How many square metres of carpet does Maya need to order for her bedroom?

A   25   C   136
B   156   D   123

20. The distance from Micah's house to school is 7 km. How many metres is this distance?

A   0.7   C   70
B   700   D   7000

STOP

ANSWER ROW   **11** Ⓐ Ⓑ Ⓒ Ⓓ   **13** Ⓐ Ⓑ Ⓒ Ⓓ   **15** Ⓐ Ⓑ Ⓒ Ⓓ   **17** Ⓐ Ⓑ Ⓒ Ⓓ   **19** Ⓐ Ⓑ Ⓒ Ⓓ
             12 Ⓐ Ⓑ Ⓒ Ⓓ   **14** Ⓐ Ⓑ Ⓒ Ⓓ   **16** Ⓐ Ⓑ Ⓒ Ⓓ   **18** Ⓐ Ⓑ Ⓒ Ⓓ   **20** Ⓐ Ⓑ Ⓒ Ⓓ

CHAPTER 9   CUMULATIVE REVIEW

Do each problem.
Find the correct answer.
Mark the space for the answer.

Part 1 Concepts

1. Which statement is true about the remainder in $24\overline{)682}$?

A   It is equal to 28.
B   It is less than 5.
C   It is greater than 12.
D   It is greater than 9.

2. Which of the following is the dollar amount for seven thousand, five hundred thirty-eight dollars and seventy-two cents?

A $738.72
B $7538.72
C $7583.72
D $7538.27

3. Which of the following represents the probability of an event?

A $\dfrac{\text{number of possible outcomes}}{\text{number of favourable outcomes}}$

B $\dfrac{\text{number of non-favourable outcome}}{\text{number of favourable outcomes}}$

C $\dfrac{\text{number of favourable outcomes}}{\text{number of possible outcomes}}$

D $\dfrac{\text{number of favourable outcomes}}{10}$

4. What do you multiply by to change 4 m to centimetres?

A   100   C   1000
B   10   D   1

Part 2 Computation

5.   487
　　−129

A   368
B   506
C   558
D   358

6.   23 694
　　+51 918

A   75 602
B   75 502
C   75 612
D   75 512

7.   569
　　×87

A   49 503
B   48 303
C   48 403
D   49 403

8. $48\overline{)850}$

A   17 r44
B   15 r20
C   17 r24
D   17 r34

9. $48.62
　　−17.83

A $30.89
B $30.79
C $39.89
D $30.97

10. What is the mean of 78, 64, 79, 63, and 76?

A   72   C   16
B   76   D   75

CUMULATIVE REVIEW

ANSWER ROW **1** Ⓐ Ⓑ Ⓒ Ⓓ   **3** Ⓐ Ⓑ Ⓒ Ⓓ   **5** Ⓐ Ⓑ Ⓒ Ⓓ   **7** Ⓐ Ⓑ Ⓒ Ⓓ   **9** Ⓐ Ⓑ Ⓒ Ⓓ
　　　　　　2 Ⓐ Ⓑ Ⓒ Ⓓ   **4** Ⓐ Ⓑ Ⓒ Ⓓ   **6** Ⓐ Ⓑ Ⓒ Ⓓ   **8** Ⓐ Ⓑ Ⓒ Ⓓ   **10** Ⓐ Ⓑ Ⓒ Ⓓ

11. 9 kg = _____ g

   A 0.009   C 900

   B 9000   D 90

12. 200 cm = _____ m

   A 2000   C 2

   B 20 000   D 200

13. What is the area of the figure shown?

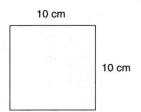

10 cm

10 cm

   A 10 cm^2 C 20 cm^2

   B 100 cm^2 D 40 cm^2

14. What is the perimeter of the figure shown?

5 mm

   A 5 mm   C   25 mm

   B 30 mm   D   35 mm

Part 3 Applications

15. Drake has 318 coins in his bank. His brother Julian has 467 coins in his bank. How many more coins does Julian have?

   A 785   C 149

   B 159   D 152

16. For lunch, Cameron bought a sandwich for $2.85, a salad for $1.70, and a fruit juice for $1.12. How much money did Cameron spend on lunch?

   A $4.67   C $4.87

   B $5.87   D $5.67

17. The pizzeria uses 17 kg of flour in each batch of dough. How many batches of dough could be made with 1598 kg of flour?

   A 194   C 97

   B 78   D 94

18. During the first seven basketball games, Dante scored the following number of points: 9, 7, 11, 5, 6, 7, and 13. What is the range of the number of points Dante scored in the first seven basketball games?

   A 7   C 8

   B 13   D 6

19. Bethany's backyard is a rectangle. It is 45 m by 59 m. What is the area of Bethany's backyard?

   A 208 m^2 C 2615 m^2

   B 2415 m^2 D 2655 m^2

20. Mr. Dean has a rectangular patio in his backyard. It is 6 m by 4 m. What is the perimeter of Mr. Dean's patio?

   A 20 m   C 16 m

   B 24 m   D 28 m

STOP

ANSWER ROW **11** Ⓐ Ⓑ Ⓒ Ⓓ **13** Ⓐ Ⓑ Ⓒ Ⓓ **15** Ⓐ Ⓑ Ⓒ Ⓓ **17** Ⓐ Ⓑ Ⓒ Ⓓ **19** Ⓐ Ⓑ Ⓒ Ⓓ

               12 Ⓐ Ⓑ Ⓒ Ⓓ **14** Ⓐ Ⓑ Ⓒ Ⓓ **16** Ⓐ Ⓑ Ⓒ Ⓓ **18** Ⓐ Ⓑ Ⓒ Ⓓ **20** Ⓐ Ⓑ Ⓒ Ⓓ

Do each problem.
Find the correct answer.
Mark the space for the answer.

Part 1 Concepts

1. Which problem would you use to find the estimated sum of 576 and 894?

A 500 + 800
B 500 + 900
C 600 + 800
D 600 + 900

2. Which of the following sets of numbers has a median of 27?

A 24, 31, 27, 29, 33
B 34, 26, 22, 27, 25
C 19, 26, 23, 21, 27
D 22, 28, 31, 34, 20

3. Which of the following units of measure would you use to measure the capacity of a bucket?

A metres
B centimetres
C litres
D grams

4. Which is another way to write $\frac{6}{9}$?

A $\frac{2}{3}$

B $\frac{9}{6}$

C $\frac{12}{15}$

D $\frac{16}{19}$

Part 2 Computation

5.   354
   $\times 2$

A 604   C 608
B 658   D 708

6. $94.36
   -7.89

A $86.47   C $86.48
B $87.57   D $97.57

7. $53\overline{)3233}$

A 68   C 71
B 61   D 53

8. $18\overline{)\$4004.64}$

A $222.47   C $220.45
B $250.01   D $222.48

9. A spinner has four sections of equal size. Two sections are yellow, one section is green, and the other section is blue. What is the probability of the spinner landing on blue?

A $\frac{1}{2}$ C $\frac{1}{3}$

B $\frac{1}{4}$ D $\frac{1}{5}$

10. 70 mm = _____ cm

A 7   C 700
B 7000   D 70 000

ANSWER ROW   **1** Ⓐ Ⓑ Ⓒ Ⓓ   **3** Ⓐ Ⓑ Ⓒ Ⓓ   **5** Ⓐ Ⓑ Ⓒ Ⓓ   **7** Ⓐ Ⓑ Ⓒ Ⓓ   **9** Ⓐ Ⓑ Ⓒ Ⓓ
              2 Ⓐ Ⓑ Ⓒ Ⓓ   **4** Ⓐ Ⓑ Ⓒ Ⓓ   **6** Ⓐ Ⓑ Ⓒ Ⓓ   **8** Ⓐ Ⓑ Ⓒ Ⓓ   **10** Ⓐ Ⓑ Ⓒ Ⓓ

PRISM MATHEMATICS
Yellow Book

CHAPTER 10
CUMULATIVE REVIEW

235

11. 4000 mL = _____ L

  A 8   C 4

  B 2   D 6

12. What is the area of the figure shown?

1 cm

3 cm

  A 1 cm^2 C 6 cm^2

  B 3 cm^2 D 8 cm^2

13. What is the greatest common factor of 18 and 32?

  A 3   C 6

  B 4   D 2

14. Rename $\frac{9}{4}$ as a mixed numeral.

  A $1\frac{4}{5}$ C $2\frac{1}{2}$

  B $1\frac{1}{2}$ D $2\frac{1}{4}$

Part 3 Applications

15. Dale golfed three games over the weekend. He scored a 67, 59, and a 61. What is the total score of Dale's three golf games?

  A 186   C 177

  B 187   D 176

16. At the grocery store, turkeys are on sale for $0.99 per kg. Mrs. Stitz bought a 12-kg turkey. How much did the turkey cost?

  A $11.76   C $9.99

  B $12.00   D $11.88

17. There are 1326 students at Glenview School. How many classes of 26 students each could there be?

  A 36   C 51

  B 61   D 26

18. Marta has a 3-kg bowling ball. How many grams is this?

  A 3   C 300

  B 30 000   D 3000

19. Mr. Carlton built a gazebo in his backyard that has five sides. Each side is 3 m long. What is the perimeter of Mr. Carlton's gazebo?

  A 15 m   C 25 m

  B 12 m   D 18 m

20. Demetre, Todd, Ken, and Dylan ordered a pizza. The pizza was cut into 12 slices. Each of them ate two pieces of pizza. In simplest form, what fraction of the pizza did the boys eat?

  A $\frac{1}{12}$ C $\frac{1}{2}$

  B $\frac{2}{12}$ D $\frac{2}{3}$

STOP

ANSWER ROW **11** Ⓐ Ⓑ Ⓒ Ⓓ **13** Ⓐ Ⓑ Ⓒ Ⓓ **15** Ⓐ Ⓑ Ⓒ Ⓓ **17** Ⓐ Ⓑ Ⓒ Ⓓ **19** Ⓐ Ⓑ Ⓒ Ⓓ

              12 Ⓐ Ⓑ Ⓒ Ⓓ **14** Ⓐ Ⓑ Ⓒ Ⓓ **16** Ⓐ Ⓑ Ⓒ Ⓓ **18** Ⓐ Ⓑ Ⓒ Ⓓ **20** Ⓐ Ⓑ Ⓒ Ⓓ

NAME _____

Do each problem.
Find the correct answer.
Mark the space for the answer.

Part 1 Concepts

1. Which of the following quotients is between 48 and 55?

A $12\overline{)418}$

B $27\overline{)1431}$

C $19\overline{)1102}$

D $31\overline{)1457}$

2. What are all the factors of 24?

A 1, 2, 4, 6, 12, 24

B 2, 4, 6, 8, 12

C 1, 2, 3, 4, 5, 6, 8, 12, 24

D 1, 2, 3, 4, 6, 8, 12, 24

3. Which problem would you use to find the estimated product of 1218 and 578?

A 1000×500

B 1200×500

C 1000×600

D 2000×600

4. What number is in the denominator of the product of $\frac{3}{7} \times \frac{3}{5}$?

A 35

B 12

C 9

D 42

Part 2 Computation

5. 312
     $\underline{\times 42}$

A 13 004

B 13 104

C 12 104

D 12 004

6. $7\overline{)9431}$

A 1347 r1

B 1343

C 1347 r3

D 1347 r2

7. $356.70
     $\underline{+343.98}$

A $699.68

B $700.68

C $700.78

D $699.68

8. What is the mode of 108, 135, 122, 106, 133, 108, and 121?

A 119   C 108

B 29   D 121

9. 3000 mL = _____ L

A 300   C 3 000 000

B 3   D 30

10. 9 cm = _____ mm

A 90   C 9000

B 900   D 9

ANSWER ROW **1** Ⓐ Ⓑ Ⓒ Ⓓ   **3** Ⓐ Ⓑ Ⓒ Ⓓ   **5** Ⓐ Ⓑ Ⓒ Ⓓ   **7** Ⓐ Ⓑ Ⓒ Ⓓ   **9** Ⓐ Ⓑ Ⓒ Ⓓ
            2 Ⓐ Ⓑ Ⓒ Ⓓ   **4** Ⓐ Ⓑ Ⓒ Ⓓ   **6** Ⓐ Ⓑ Ⓒ Ⓓ   **8** Ⓐ Ⓑ Ⓒ Ⓓ   **10** Ⓐ Ⓑ Ⓒ Ⓓ

11. 5 m = _____ cm

  A 500   C 50

  B 5000   D 5

12. What is the perimeter of the figure shown?

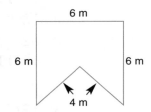

  A 22 m   C 32 m

  B 20 m   D 26 m

13. Change $5\frac{6}{7}$ to a fraction.

  A $\frac{41}{7}$ C $\frac{30}{7}$

  B $\frac{36}{7}$ D $\frac{35}{7}$

14. $\frac{5}{9} \times \frac{6}{10}$

  A $\frac{50}{39}$ C $\frac{1}{3}$

  B $\frac{3}{5}$ D $\frac{4}{5}$

Part 3 Applications

15. Jacqueline went shopping at the mall. She bought a dress for $54.83, a pair of shoes for $21.95, and a necklace for $17.30. How much money did Jacqueline spend at the mall?

  A $94.08   C $83.08

  B $93.08   D $84.08

16. The warehouse inventory shows that there are 5778 books in the warehouse. There are 18 books in each box. How many boxes of books should there be in the warehouse?

  A 321   C 521

  B 354   D 368

17. Last week, Silvia kept track of the number of kilometres she drove each day of the week. She drove the following number of kilometres Sunday through Saturday: 5, 28, 34, 28, 33, 41, 13. What is the mean number of kilometres Silvia drove each day last week?

  A 26   C 28

  B 41   D 182

18. On Saturday, Calvin ran in a 15-km race. How many metres was the race?

  A 1500   C 15 000

  B 0.015   D 150

19. On a math quiz, Adrian scored an $\frac{18}{20}$. In simplest form, what was Adrian's score on the math quiz?

  A $\frac{6}{10}$ C $\frac{3}{10}$

  B $\frac{9}{10}$ D $\frac{1}{2}$

20. Miliya needs 8 bows. It takes her $\frac{3}{4}$ min to make each one. How long does it take her to make all the bows?

  A 8 min   C $6\frac{3}{4}$ min

  B 7 min   D 6 min

STOP

ANSWER ROW **11** Ⓐ Ⓑ Ⓒ Ⓓ **13** Ⓐ Ⓑ Ⓒ Ⓓ **15** Ⓐ Ⓑ Ⓒ Ⓓ **17** Ⓐ Ⓑ Ⓒ Ⓓ **19** Ⓐ Ⓑ Ⓒ Ⓓ

  12 Ⓐ Ⓑ Ⓒ Ⓓ **14** Ⓐ Ⓑ Ⓒ Ⓓ **16** Ⓐ Ⓑ Ⓒ Ⓓ **18** Ⓐ Ⓑ Ⓒ Ⓓ **20** Ⓐ Ⓑ Ⓒ Ⓓ

NAME _____

Do each problem.
Find the correct answer.
Mark the space for the answer.

Part 1 Concepts

1. In $3291.54, what number is in the tenths place?

   A 1 C 4
   B 9 D 5

2. How many digits are in the product of 648×92?

   A 2 C 5
   B 3 D 6

3. When writing $\frac{16}{24}$ in simplest form, by what number do you divide the numerator and denominator?

   A the greatest common factor of 16 and 24
   B the sum of 16 and 24
   C the product of 16 and 24
   D the value of the denominator, 24

4. What number is in the numerator of the sum of $\frac{1}{5} + \frac{2}{3}$?

   A 13 C 2
   B 3 D 15

5. Which number is the divisor in $513\overline{)8461}$?

   A 8461 C 16
   B 513 D 16 r3

Part 2 Computation

6. $\begin{array}{r} 45\,678 \\ +82\,902 \end{array}$

   A 128 570
   B 129 570
   C 129 580
   D 128 580

7. $89\overline{)10\,324}$

   A 113
   B 116
   C 112
   D 115

8. $\begin{array}{r} \$592.46 \\ -370.95 \end{array}$

   A $963.41
   B $222.51
   C $863.41
   D $221.51

9. $4\,\text{kg} = $ _____ g

   A 400 C 40 000
   B 4000 D 4

2 m

17 m

10. What is the area of the figure shown?

   A $34\,\text{m}^2$ C $38\,\text{m}^2$
   B $36\,\text{m}^2$ D $40\,\text{m}^2$

GO

ANSWER ROW   1 Ⓐ Ⓑ Ⓒ Ⓓ   3 Ⓐ Ⓑ Ⓒ Ⓓ   5 Ⓐ Ⓑ Ⓒ Ⓓ   7 Ⓐ Ⓑ Ⓒ Ⓓ   9 Ⓐ Ⓑ Ⓒ Ⓓ

2 Ⓐ Ⓑ Ⓒ Ⓓ   4 Ⓐ Ⓑ Ⓒ Ⓓ   6 Ⓐ Ⓑ Ⓒ Ⓓ   8 Ⓐ Ⓑ Ⓒ Ⓓ   10 Ⓐ Ⓑ Ⓒ Ⓓ

PRISM MATHEMATICS
Yellow Book

CHAPTER 12
CUMULATIVE REVIEW

239

CUMULATIVE REVIEW

11. Write in $3\frac{10}{12}$ simplest form.

    A $3\frac{5}{6}$ C $3\frac{5}{12}$

    B $3\frac{2}{3}$ D $3\frac{1}{2}$

12. $9 \times \frac{5}{6}$

    A $9\frac{4}{5}$

    B $9\frac{5}{6}$

    C $7\frac{1}{2}$

    D $7\frac{1}{3}$

13. $8\frac{3}{16}$
$+5\frac{7}{8}$

    A $14\frac{3}{16}$

    B $13\frac{5}{8}$

    C $13\frac{1}{16}$

    D $14\frac{1}{16}$

Part 3 Applications

Use this graph to answer question 13.

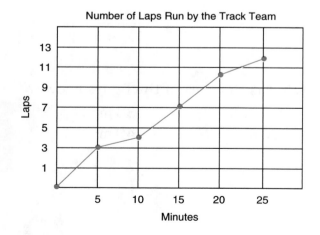

Number of Laps Run by the Track Team

14. How many laps did the track team run in 15 min?

    A 7   C 8

    B 10   D 3

15. Ming's car has a 48-L gas tank. A full tank of gas will last for 672 km. How many kilometres can Ming's car be driven for each litre of gas?

    A 30   C 28

    B 14   D 10

16. Mr. Benton is painting three rooms of his house. He calculated that he will be painting $128\,\text{m}^2$. Each can of paint will cover $9\,\text{m}^2$. How many cans of paint will Mr. Benton need to paint all three rooms?

    A 30   C 15

    B 119   D 14

17. Picture frame A's perimeter is $2\frac{1}{2}$ times picture frame B's perimeter, which is $3\frac{3}{4}$ times picture C's perimeter. How many times picture C's perimeter is picture A's perimeter?

    A $6\frac{1}{4}$ C $1\frac{1}{4}$

    B $9\frac{3}{8}$ D $1\frac{1}{2}$

18. Peter can jump $1\frac{7}{8}$ times as far as Maria, who can jump $3\frac{1}{3}$ times as far as Jack. How many times as far as Jack can Peter jump?

    A $3\frac{5}{24}$ C $\frac{13}{24}$

    B $2\frac{1}{2}$ D $\frac{32}{45}$

STOP

ANSWER ROW **11** Ⓐ Ⓑ Ⓒ Ⓓ **13** Ⓐ Ⓑ Ⓒ Ⓓ **15** Ⓐ Ⓑ Ⓒ Ⓓ **17** Ⓐ Ⓑ Ⓒ Ⓓ
            12 Ⓐ Ⓑ Ⓒ Ⓓ **14** Ⓐ Ⓑ Ⓒ Ⓓ **16** Ⓐ Ⓑ Ⓒ Ⓓ **18** Ⓐ Ⓑ Ⓒ Ⓓ

NAME _____

Do each problem.
Find the correct answer.
Mark the space for the answer.

Part 1 Concepts

1. Which of the following addition problems has a sum closest to 1300?

A 964 + 137
B 437 + 981
C 557 + 820
D 615 + 693

2. Which of the following is true?

A $1\,cm = 100\,m$
B $1000\,g = 1\,kg$
C $1\,L = 1000\,kL$
D $1\,km = 100\,cm$

3. Which of the following numbers is not prime?

A 7
B 5
C 11
D 9

4. When solving the problem $\frac{13}{16} - \frac{3}{8}$, how should you rename the problem?

A $\frac{13}{16} - \frac{6}{16}$
C $\frac{13}{16} - \frac{3}{16}$
B $\frac{6}{8} - \frac{3}{8}$
D $\frac{13}{16} - \frac{11}{16}$

Part 2 Computation

5.
$$\begin{array}{r} 16 \\ 9 \\ 23 \\ +75 \end{array}$$

A 103
B 123
C 204
D 120

6.
$$\begin{array}{r} 785 \\ \times 546 \end{array}$$

A 11 775
B 1331
C 382 980
D 428 610

7. $21\overline{)\$18.69}$

A $0.89
B $8.13
C $0.91
D $8.90

8. $6\,kL =$ _____ L

A 6
B 600
C 60
D 6000

9. A coin is tossed. What is the probability of it landing on tails?

A 1
B 2
C $\frac{1}{2}$
D $\frac{1}{4}$

10. $\frac{3}{4} \times \frac{7}{8}$

A $\frac{24}{28}$
B $\frac{10}{12}$
C $1\frac{5}{8}$
D $\frac{21}{32}$

 GO

CUMULATIVE REVIEW

ANSWER ROW **1** Ⓐ Ⓑ Ⓒ Ⓓ   **3** Ⓐ Ⓑ Ⓒ Ⓓ   **5** Ⓐ Ⓑ Ⓒ Ⓓ   **7** Ⓐ Ⓑ Ⓒ Ⓓ   **9** Ⓐ Ⓑ Ⓒ Ⓓ

2 Ⓐ Ⓑ Ⓒ Ⓓ   **4** Ⓐ Ⓑ Ⓒ Ⓓ   **6** Ⓐ Ⓑ Ⓒ Ⓓ   **8** Ⓐ Ⓑ Ⓒ Ⓓ   **10** Ⓐ Ⓑ Ⓒ Ⓓ

11. Write $\frac{26}{3}$ as a mixed numeral.

    A $8\frac{2}{3}$ C $8\frac{1}{3}$

    B $3\frac{1}{3}$ D $9\frac{2}{3}$

12. $\frac{3}{5} \times \frac{4}{9}$

    A $\frac{1}{2}$ C $\frac{20}{27}$

    B $\frac{6}{7}$ D $\frac{4}{15}$

13. $7\frac{3}{4}$
$+6\frac{3}{8}$

    A $13\frac{3}{4}$

    B $14\frac{1}{8}$

    C $13\frac{7}{8}$

    D $14\frac{3}{4}$

14. $\frac{5}{6}$
$-\frac{1}{9}$

    A $\frac{13}{18}$

    B $1\frac{1}{3}$

    C $\frac{17}{18}$

    D $\frac{4}{9}$

Part 3 Applications

15. Benjamin bought a football that cost $14.69. He paid with a $20 bill. How much change did Benjamin get back?

    A $34.69   C $6.31

    B $5.31   D $16.41

16. Gabrielle works 13 h a week at her part-time job. How many hours does Gabrielle work in 52 weeks?

    A 208   C 65

    B 676   D 715

17. A basketball court is 28 m by 15 m. What is the area of the basketball court?

    A 420 m^2 C 86 m^2

    B 210 m^2 D 42 m^2

18. Shalesha bought $\frac{3}{4}$ of a whole turkey. She used $\frac{1}{5}$ of the turkey to make sandwiches. How much of a whole turkey did Shalesha use on her sandwiches?

    A $\frac{4}{9}$ C $\frac{19}{20}$

    B $\frac{3}{20}$ D $\frac{11}{20}$

19. Kenyon and Miguel ordered a pizza. Kenyon ate $\frac{1}{4}$ of the pizza. Miguel ate $\frac{1}{3}$ of the pizza. How much of the pizza did Kenyon and Miguel eat?

    A $\frac{1}{12}$ C $\frac{2}{7}$

    B $\frac{3}{20}$ D $\frac{7}{12}$

20. Meagan ran $9\frac{1}{2}$ laps on Monday and $6\frac{3}{4}$ laps on Tuesday. How many more laps did she run on Tuesday than on Monday?

    A $16\frac{1}{4}$ C $3\frac{3}{4}$

    B $2\frac{3}{4}$ D $3\frac{1}{4}$

STOP

ANSWER ROW   **11** Ⓐ Ⓑ Ⓒ Ⓓ   **13** Ⓐ Ⓑ Ⓒ Ⓓ   **15** Ⓐ Ⓑ Ⓒ Ⓓ   **17** Ⓐ Ⓑ Ⓒ Ⓓ   **19** Ⓐ Ⓑ Ⓒ Ⓓ

                12 Ⓐ Ⓑ Ⓒ Ⓓ   **14** Ⓐ Ⓑ Ⓒ Ⓓ   **16** Ⓐ Ⓑ Ⓒ Ⓓ   **18** Ⓐ Ⓑ Ⓒ Ⓓ   **20** Ⓐ Ⓑ Ⓒ Ⓓ

NAME _____

Do each problem.
Find the correct answer.
Mark the space for the answer.

Part 1 Concepts

1. What is the estimated quotient of $9\overline{)263}$?

   A 20   C 40

   B 30   D 55

2. Which of the following numbers is not a factor of 36?

   A 3   C 8

   B 6   D 12

3. Which of the following fractions is not equivalent to $\frac{12}{18}$?

   A $\frac{2}{3}$ C $\frac{4}{6}$

   B $\frac{6}{9}$ D $\frac{3}{4}$

4. Which of the following is a quadrilateral?

   A pentagon

   B triangle

   C trapezoid

   D octagon

5. Which of the following numbers is prime?

   A 7   C 36

   B 49   D 15

Part 2 Computation

6. 657
     $\times 89$

   A 58 473

   B 11 169

   C 59 773

   D 17 106

7. $40\overline{)2023}$

   A 51 r17

   B 50 r20

   C 102 r23

   D 50 r23

8. What is the mean of $325, $312, $367, $354, and $312?

   A $334   C $312

   B $55   D $325

9. 800 cm = _____ m

   A 80   C 0.8

   B 80 000   D 8

10. What is the volume of the figure shown?

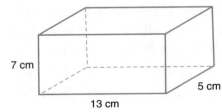

7 cm   13 cm   5 cm

   A 150 cm^3 C 5 cm^3

   B 455 cm^3 D 910 cm^3

ANSWER ROW   **1** Ⓐ Ⓑ Ⓒ Ⓓ   **3** Ⓐ Ⓑ Ⓒ Ⓓ   **5** Ⓐ Ⓑ Ⓒ Ⓓ   **7** Ⓐ Ⓑ Ⓒ Ⓓ   **9** Ⓐ Ⓑ Ⓒ Ⓓ

               2 Ⓐ Ⓑ Ⓒ Ⓓ   **4** Ⓐ Ⓑ Ⓒ Ⓓ   **6** Ⓐ Ⓑ Ⓒ Ⓓ   **8** Ⓐ Ⓑ Ⓒ Ⓓ   **10** Ⓐ Ⓑ Ⓒ Ⓓ

11. $\frac{1}{3} \times 4\frac{1}{2}$

    A $4\frac{1}{6}$ C $1\frac{1}{6}$

    B $1\frac{1}{2}$ D $1\frac{2}{3}$

12.

    A $2\frac{2}{9}$

    B $1\frac{2}{9}$

    C $2\frac{8}{9}$

    D $1\frac{1}{3}$

13. Name the figure shown.

    A line segment XY

    B line X

    C line XY

    D line Y

14. Name the figure shown.

    A triangle

    B pentagon

    C hexagon

    D quadrilateral

Part 3 Applications

15. On vacation, Lamar bought 3 T-shirts. Each T-shirt cost $13.98. How much did Lamar spend on the T-shirts he bought while on vacation?

    A $27.96   C $41.94

    B $37.31   D $39.74

16. There are 20 736 students attending 32 different schools in a school district. Suppose the same number of students attend each school. How many students attend each school?

    A 745   C 597

    B 651   D 648

17. Elsa bought 3 L of fruit juice. How many millilitres of fruit juice did Elsa buy?

    A 3000 mL   C 30 000 mL

    B 300 mL   D 30 mL

18. It takes Isaac $5\frac{1}{2}$ h to drive to his parents' house, and $3\frac{1}{3}$ h to drive to his grandparents' house. How many more hours does it take Isaac to drive to his parents' house?

    A 2   C $2\frac{1}{3}$

    B $2\frac{1}{6}$ D $1\frac{1}{6}$

19. Mitch stocks the cereal aisle at the grocery store. Which term best describes the shape of a cereal box?

    A circle   C rectangular prism

    B cube   D pentagon

20. Kim read for $1\frac{1}{2}$ h. Alex read for $\frac{3}{4}$ h. How much longer did Kim read?

    A $\frac{1}{2}$ h   C $\frac{3}{4}$ h

    B $1\frac{1}{2}$ h   D $\frac{1}{4}$ h

STOP

ANSWER ROW **11** Ⓐ Ⓑ Ⓒ Ⓓ **13** Ⓐ Ⓑ Ⓒ Ⓓ **15** Ⓐ Ⓑ Ⓒ Ⓓ **17** Ⓐ Ⓑ Ⓒ Ⓓ **19** Ⓐ Ⓑ Ⓒ Ⓓ

              12 Ⓐ Ⓑ Ⓒ Ⓓ **14** Ⓐ Ⓑ Ⓒ Ⓓ **16** Ⓐ Ⓑ Ⓒ Ⓓ **18** Ⓐ Ⓑ Ⓒ Ⓓ **20** Ⓐ Ⓑ Ⓒ Ⓓ

ALGEBRA READINESS
Missing Term—Addition

Subtraction Property of Equality: If you subtract the same number from each side of an equation, the two sides remain equal.

Find the value of the missing term in the equation $x + 4 = 9$ using the Subtraction Property of Equality.

$$x + 4 = 9$$

To undo the addition of 4, subtract 4 from both sides of the equation.

$$x + 4 - 4 = 9 - 4$$

$$x + 0 = 5$$

$$x = 5$$

Circle the operation you should perform on both sides of the equation to find the missing term.

1. $n + 2 = 6$ subtract 6   (subtract 2)   add 2

2. $5 + y = 11$ add 5   subtract 11   subtract 5

3. $x + 8 = 10$ subtract 8   add 8   subtract 10

4. $4 + w = 7$ subtract 7   subtract 4   add 4

Find the value of the missing term in each equation.

5. $x + 3 = 8$ _____5_____ $m + 2 = 6$ _____

6. $7 + y = 11$ _____ $4 + d = 7$ _____

7. $n + 2 = 12$ _____ $x + 9 = 14$ _____

8. $8 + w = 15$ _____ $6 + z = 16$ _____

ALGEBRA READINESS

ALGEBRA READINESS
Missing Term—Subtraction

Addition Property of Equality: If you add the same number to each side of an equation, the two sides remain equal.

Find the value of the missing term in the equation $x - 3 = 5$ using the Addition Property of Equality.

$$x - 3 = 5$$

To undo the subtraction of 3, add 3 to both sides of the equation.

$$x - 3 + 3 = 5 + 3$$

$$x + 0 = 8$$

$$x = 8$$

Circle the operation you should perform on both sides of the equation to find the missing term.

1. $n - 4 = 3$	add 3	subtract 4	(add 4)
2. $y - 7 = 2$	add 7	add 2	subtract 2
3. $d - 3 = 8$	subtract 3	add 3	add 8
4. $x - 2 = 11$	add 11	subtract 2	add 2

Find the value of the missing term in each equation.

5. $m - 8 = 2$ _____10_____ $d - 4 = 8$ _____

6. $x - 3 = 2$ _____ $z - 6 = 3$ _____

7. $y - 1 = 7$ _____ $n - 7 = 7$ _____

8. $n - 5 = 6$ _____ $x - 2 = 9$ _____

ALGEBRA READINESS
Missing Term—Multiplication

Division Property of Equality: If you divide each side of an equation by the same non-zero number, the two sides remain equal.

Find the value of the missing term in the equation $4 \times n = 12$ using the Division Property of Equality.

$$4 \times n = 12$$

To undo the multiplication of 4, divide by 4 on both sides of the equation.

$$\frac{4 \times n}{4} = \frac{12}{4}$$

$$n = 3$$

Circle the operation you should perform on both sides of the equation to find the missing term.

1. $7 \times x = 28$ multiply by 7   (divide by 7)   divide by 28

2. $m \times 5 = 25$ divide by 5   multiply by 5   divide by 25

3. $3 \times y = 27$ divide by 27   divide by 3   multiply by 3

4. $n \times 8 = 48$ divide by 48   multiply by 8   divide by 8

Find the value of the missing term in each equation.

5. $3 \times n = 24$ __8__ $8 \times w = 32$ _____

6. $w \times 5 = 45$ _____ $m \times 9 = 18$ _____

7. $x \times 7 = 14$ _____ $3 \times d = 33$ _____

8. $6 \times y = 36$ _____ $z \times 7 = 63$ _____

PRISM MATHEMATICS
Yellow Book

ALGEBRA READINESS
Missing Term—Multiplication
247

ALGEBRA
READINESS

ALGEBRA READINESS
Missing Term—Division

Multiplication Property of Equality: If you multiply each side of an equation by the same number, the two sides remain equal.

Find the value of the missing term in the equation $\frac{n}{3} = 6$ using the Multiplication Property of Equality.

$$\frac{n}{3} = 6$$

To undo the division by 3, multiply by 3 on both sides of the equation.

$$\frac{n}{3} \times 3 = 6 \times 3$$

$$n = 18$$

Circle the operation you should perform on both sides of the equation to find the missing term.

1. $\frac{x}{4} = 6$ (multiply by 4)   divide by 4   multiply by 6

2. $\frac{a}{2} = 9$ multiply by 9   multiply by 2   divide by 2

3. $\frac{w}{5} = 6$ divide by 5   multiply by 6   multiply by 5

4. $\frac{n}{6} = 8$ divide by 8   multiply by 8   multiply by 6

Find the value of the missing term in each equation.

5. $\frac{n}{2} = 7$ _____14_____ $\frac{w}{7} = 8$ _____

6. $\frac{x}{6} = 4$ _____ $\frac{x}{5} = 7$ _____

7. $\frac{m}{8} = 5$ _____ $\frac{n}{12} = 10$ _____

8. $\frac{a}{3} = 12$ _____ $\frac{x}{9} = 8$ _____

ALGEBRA READINESS
Mixed Missing Term

Circle the operation you should perform on both sides of the equation to find the missing term.

1. $7 \times n = 49$ multiply by 7   (divide by 7)   divide by 49

2. $a + 6 = 10$ subtract 6   add 6   subtract 10

3. $x - 3 = 8$ subtract 3   add 8   add 3

4. $\dfrac{w}{4} = 9$ divide by 4   multiply by 4   multiply by 9

5. $8 + y = 13$ subtract 8   subtract 13   add 8

6. $m \times 4 = 48$ multiply by 4   divide by 4   multiply by 48

Find the value of the missing term in each equation.

7. $\dfrac{w}{6} = 5$ ___30___ $d - 7 = 8$ _____

8. $8 + a = 12$ _____ $\dfrac{n}{4} = 7$ _____

9. $3 \times x = 21$ _____ $m - 3 = 15$ _____

10. $y - 5 = 4$ _____ $\dfrac{x}{5} = 12$ _____

11. $9 + n = 16$ _____ $w \times 8 = 64$ _____

ALGEBRA READINESS
Function Tables

A **function** is a rule that relates two variables. A function states that for each value of one variable, there is exactly one value related to the other variable.

For example, $y = 4 + x$ is a function. For each value of x, there is exactly one value of y. To find each value of y for a given value of x, add 4 to the given value for x.

A **function table** helps you organize the values of a function. For each entry in the first column, there is exactly one entry in the second column.

Shown is the function table for $y = 4 + x$.

The x-values in the function table are 1, 2, 3, and 4. To find each y-value, add 4 to each x-value.

x	y
1	5
2	6
3	7
4	8

$1 + 4 = 5$

$2 + 4 = 6$

$3 + 4 = 7$

$4 + 4 = 8$

Complete each function table for the given function.

1. $y = 2 + x$

x	y
1	3
2	
3	
4	

$y = 7 + x$

x	y
1	
2	
3	
4	

2. $y = x - 3$

x	y
4	
5	
6	
7	

$y = x - 5$

x	y
10	
15	
20	
25	

ALGEBRA READINESS
Function Tables

Complete each function table for the given function.

3. $y = 2 \times x$

x	y
1	2
2	
3	
4	

$y = 6 \times x$

x	y
1	
2	
3	
4	

4. $y = \dfrac{x}{3}$

x	y
3	
6	
9	
12	

$y = \dfrac{x}{5}$

x	y
5	
10	
15	
20	

Create a function table for each function. Use the given values
of x in the function table.

5. $y = x + 3$; $x = 1, 2, 3, 4$

$y = x - 4$; $x = 5, 6, 7, 8$

6. $y = 3 \times x$; $x = 1, 2, 3, 4$

$y = \dfrac{x}{2}$; $x = 2, 4, 6, 8$

ALGEBRA READINESS
Number Patterns

To determine the pattern relating a set of numbers, look at the relationship between each pair of consecutive numbers.

What are the next three numbers in the pattern 1, 4, 7, 10, 13, . . .?

Determine what operation is performed to get from one number to the next number in the pattern.

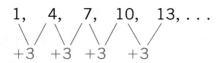

$$1, \quad 4, \quad 7, \quad 10, \quad 13, \ldots$$
$$+3 \quad +3 \quad +3 \quad +3$$

To get from one number to the next in the pattern, 3 is added.

Add 3 to 13 to get the 6th number in the pattern. $13 + 3 = 16$

Add 3 to 16 to get the 7th number in the pattern. $16 + 3 = 19$

Add 3 to 19 to get the 8th number in the pattern. $19 + 3 = 22$

The next three numbers in the pattern are ____16, 19, 22____.

Find the next three numbers of each pattern.

a

b

1. 2, 7, 12, 17, 22, . . . _____27_____   1, 3, 5, 7, 9, . . .   _____

2. 1, 2, 4, 7, 11, 16, . . . _____   84, 78, 72, 66, 60, . . . _____

3. 2, 6, 10, 14, 18, . . . _____   5, 10, 20, 35, 55, . . .   _____

4. 108, 96, 84, 72, . . . _____   2, 4, 8, 16, 32, . . .   _____

5. 1, 3, 9, 27, . . .   _____   320, 160, 80, 40, . . .   _____